— Doris J. Shallcross —

Teaching
Creative
Behavior

*How to Teach Creativity
to Children of All Ages*

A SPECTRUM BOOK

Prentice-Hall, Inc., *Englewood Cliffs, N.J. 07632*

Library of Congress Cataloging in Publication Data

Shallcross, Doris J
  Teaching creative behavior.

  (A Spectrum Book)
  Bibliography: p.
  Includes index.
  1. Creative thinking (Education)   2. Activity
programs in education.   I. Title.
LB1062.S46   370.15'2   80-21728
ISBN 0-13-891945-3
ISBN 0-13-891937-2 (pbk.)

Editorial/Production Supervision by *Heath Lynn Silberfeld*
Illustrations by *Terez Waldoch*
Manufacturing buyer: *Cathie Lenard*

To Ethel Ruth Shallcross, my mother,
and the late John William Shallcross, my father
—creative people themselves
and supportive of others who would be

© 1981 by Prentice-Hall, Inc., Englewood Cliffs, New Jersey 07632

A SPECTRUM BOOK

10 9 8 7 6 5 4 3 2 1

Printed in the United States of America

PRENTICE-HALL INTERNATIONAL, INC., *London*
PRENTICE-HALL OF AUSTRALIA PTY. LIMITED, *Sydney*
PRENTICE-HALL OF CANADA, LTD., *Toronto*
PRENTICE-HALL OF INDIA PRIVATE LIMITED, *New Delhi*
PRENTICE-HALL OF JAPAN, INC., *Tokyo*
PRENTICE-HALL OF SOUTHEAST ASIA PTE. LTD., *Singapore*
WHITEHALL BOOKS LIMITED, WELLINGTON, *New Zealand*

Contents

Foreword

The elusive dream of personal fulfillment and creative expression has been a never-ending search of human beings throughout time. With our current increased technology and advanced achievement level, the search has become more possible and at the same time more precarious.

We are always learning more about the nature of the human being as the life sciences of biology, psychology, sociology, and anthropology continue to explore their disciplines. Yet with the great human and social problems that these very technological advances have often created, many people feel troubled and overwhelmed.

This is an important book in that it will aid teachers and laymen in searching deeply within themselves for personal meaning. It will also enable readers to explore their understanding of the nature of creativity and its application to daily living.

Sir Hubert Read said that destructiveness and creativity are opposing forces in the mind. This book focuses on the concept of creativity as a constructive force. This constructing is described as happening in a cooperative fashion, with emphasis on the building of a spirit of community.

Approaches to creativity and to creative teaching abound, and yet many of them fail because they are too contrived, intentional, and self-conscious. Dr. Shallcross realizes this, and her book helps the individual experience the creative process through engaging exercises and the "processing" of material. She defines *processing* as the application of cognitive thought to the feelings that were shared in the activity.

In this way, the teacher will grasp the fundamental attitude of creativity—the blending of the self (feelings) and the prepared mind (inspiration and work).

Dr. Shallcross's emphasis on the creative climate is excellent, because the teachers must provide the psychological climate for creation to take place. The teacher must set the creative pattern in which the creativity can flow. This book demonstrates step by step how to evoke creative behavior.

In the words of Miss Sylvia Ashton Warner, a great creative teacher, Dr. Shallcross is teaching education in its truest sense—the drawing out of another mind its creative response.

Today's school must be redirected to its original commitment to the whole individual and to provide opportunities for real change to take place. Creativity has been a persistent and recurrent issue throughout the history of education, yet the idea of creative ways of teaching has not been given a fair chance to prove its worth. With the hue and cry to return to the basics, and the classroom teacher struggling to apply the mass of material available on creativity, books such as this one, which is imaginative, informed, and above all a tool for how to set the conditions for creative teaching and learning, are a welcome addition to the educational literature.

It is my hope that the creative use of this book will help more individuals to realize fully their dream of personal fulfillment and creative expression.

Creativity is a precious commodity, and creative people are the ones who will make the great advances in medicine and science, literature and art and move our civilization forward. *Teaching Creative Behavior* could easily be dedicated to all the creative teachers in the world, for it speaks of the essence of the creative teacher.

> Dorothy A. Sisk
> Professor, Educational Psychology
> University of South Florida, Tampa
> Formerly Director of the Office of Gifted and Talented,
> United States Office of Education

Grateful acknowledgments are extended to those who have influenced and encouraged my work in creative behavior. My original mentors were the late Alex F. Osborn, who gave me my initial impetus, and Sidney J. Parnes, whose inspiration and support have been sustaining. Many of my other colleagues in the Creative Education Foundation have been positive influences for me, especially Robert Eberle, John C. Gowan, J.P. Guilford, George T.L. Ainsworth-Land, Donald MacKinnon, Dorothy A. Sisk, E. Paul Torrance, and Frank E. Williams.

I am also very indebted to Terez Waldoch for the illustrations in this text, and to both her and Louise Kanus for both their reactions to the text and their encouragement throughout the years. Special thanks to Sister Sharon Waldoch for her thoughtful comments on the book, and to Marianne Galvin for her research efforts.

And, finally, to the many students, teachers, and other professional groups with whom I have worked go my thanks for proving that teaching to evoke creative behavior really works.

ABOUT THE AUTHOR

Doris Shallcross has been teaching in the field of creative behavior for fifteen years. She has worked with children and adolescents and other preservice and in-service teachers. Dr. Shallcross is presently an assistant professor of education with the Division of Home Economics, University of Massachusetts, Amherst.

Creativity: Everybody's Business

FOR STARTERS . . . TRY THIS

Fold your hands. Notice which thumb is on top. Now switch all of your fingers so that the other thumb is on top.

How does that feel? Probably awkward, uncomfortable. Cross your arms. Then cross them in the opposite way from the way you usually do. Try the same thing with crossing your legs.

You've been asked to assume positions that are the opposite of what is usual or comfortable for you in a physical sense. Your venture into this book will ask you to do the same kinds of things in a mental sense. Perhaps you'll experience some initial discomfort or frustration, for the intent here is to jar you out of mental lethargy and to develop the creative potential within you.

THE CREATIVE PERSON

Creativity is not the exclusive posession of a chosen few, the Mozarts, the Rembrandts, the Einsteins. Their talents might be more obvious and grandiose, but their kind do not have a corner on the market. Creativity is in all of us. It is that ability that raises humanity above the other living species in our world. Creative abilities exist in varying degrees among us, as do other kinds of intelligence. It is a matter of getting those abilities to surface and making them work for us.

Documented studies of highly creative people (MacKinnon, Barron) have demonstrated that these individuals have been able to discipline their minds, that is, they have learned self-discipline, toward their own creative development. Some major conclusions drawn from studying these individuals are that mature, highly creative people

1. seek to open their minds and the minds of others to the new

2. operate as integral wholes, that is, they think for themselves, using themselves as a source

3. seek to sustain this opening up of their own minds and integrating what is outside themselves for long periods of time

4. seek resolutions by means of a sustained sequence, which moves back and forth, from within themselves to outside themselves

This concept has been depicted by the sign of infinity. (See page 3.)

Creative individuals stay open to all that is external, integrating what they find outside themselves with the internal. The most important element of this concept is that highly creative individuals respect themselves as a source as much as they respect external sources. They have the self-confidence that they, too, can contribute to the world of knowledge.

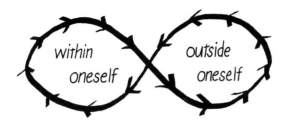

The concept of a biological basis of creativity in all of us is generally accepted. Markberry distinguishes between biological creativity—in all animals—and psychological creativity—in human beings exclusively. She claims that psychological creativity gives each individual the power of producing various, personally meaningful kinds of new products outside of his or her physical self.

Our own attitudes are the key to the realization of the potentialities within us. To put it very simplistically, we approach a task either negatively or positively. We say to ourselves, "It can't be done," or else we say, "In what ways might it be done?" A positive attitude is crucial, and that comes through the development of a positive self-concept.

The Human Potential Movement of the past two decades has done more to influence the Creative Education Movement than many people realize. In my view, it is the sense of self emphasized by the Human Potential Movement that allows one the feeling of personal freedom to be creatively expressive. Maslow talked about self-actualization. On his "hierarchy of human needs," creativity and self-realization are at the top of the scale. The top of the scale is not in the same place for everyone. What satisfies the need for self-fulfillment for one person can be drastically different for another. The theoretical person is capable of the type of abstract thought that can solve the problems that plague all humankind, yet he or she still needs to rely on the kind of plumber who takes pride in his or her work and can solve a different kind of problem. Creativity is everybody's business.

SOME HISTORICAL
PERSPECTIVES OF CREATIVITY
IN EDUCATION

Prior to the 1950s there were a few individuals who paved the way for the possibility of empirical research and subsequent program development in the field of creativity: F. Galton studied hereditary genius; G. Wallas designed a model for describing steps that were regarded as creative processes; in the late 1930s Catherine Patrick subjected Wallas's model to some experimental examination; J. Rossman provided a similar model after studying the reported performance of a large number of American inventors; and Harvey Lehman studied the biographies of productive people in many fields of activity in order to determine the relations of both quality and quantity of creative output to age during adult years.

During the 1950s a flurry of activity began in regard to creativity. Research centers devoted large portions of their efforts to the subject and to developmental use of new knowledge about creative persons and creative processes. One of the most notable centers to evolve at that time was the Aptitudes Research Project at the University of Southern California, where J. P. Guilford has done his work. The primary goal of this project was to understand human intelligence in general, including the thinking processes of individuals when they are in the act of creative production. Guilford and his associates were determined to substantiate their hypothesis that one of the most important aspects of intelligence is creative thinking ability.

The approach of the Aptitudes Research Project was to study individual differences in the performances of educated people in general, with the assumption that whatever the essential functions of creative thinkers are, they are shared to some degree by most of humankind. They devised tests that succeeded in identifying certain creative abilities that then served as the major thrust for subsequent studies in the field. The abilities they identified are sensitivity, four kinds of fluency (word, ideational, associational, and expressional), and two kinds of flexibility (spontaneous and adaptive).

Under the leadership of Donald MacKinnon and Frank

Barron, a different approach was taken at the Institute for Personality Research and Assessment at the University of California at Berkeley. Their goal was to study people who are recognized to be creatively productive in several fields in order to determine what traits or qualities set them apart from educated humanity in general. To a very extensive degree they assessed leaders in the fields of writing, architecture, administration, and mathematics.

E. Paul Torrance at the University of Minnesota studied the creative performances of children as well as those of teachers who attempted to teach creative thinking. In addition to relating creative performance to ages of children and adolescents, Torrance made important contributions relating creative performance to environmental conditions that influence it.

At the University of Utah, Calvin Taylor and his associates developed a biographical inventory for indicating creative promise in the sciences and sponsored significant conferences on creative scientific talent.

In the early 1950s Alex Osborn published his book *Applied Imagination,* founded the Creative Education Foundation, and in 1954 sponsored the first annual Creative Problem-Solving Institute in Buffalo, New York. Osborn's work has been carried on by Sidney J. Parnes. The Institute marked its twenty-fifth anniversary in 1979. The Foundation produces the *Journal of Creative Behavior,* the only periodical devoted exclusively to creativity.

The federal government took its cue from these important leaders of the 1950s and enacted, under the Elementary and Secondary Schools Act in the 1960s, Title III, Programs for the Advancement of Creativity in Education. The 1970s have seen the federal government supporting programs for gifted children and adolescents. The majority of these programs stress the development of creative talents.

Important implications can be found for creativity programs in education in the recent discoveries in regard to left-brain/right-brain orientation. Public schools traditionally have emphasized development of left-brain functions, that is, of language processes and on the logical, sequential processing of information. Research findings have indicated that the learning styles of some people are right-brained, that is, they absorb information best through visual or intuitive means. These findings lend credence to the surge of interest of the past two decades in Eastern philosophies, which elevate the intuitive function, and remind us that the intuitive is vital to the learning process of many individuals.

two

Creativity: Product, Process, Personality, Environment

Creativity is a most elusive term. Volumes have been written in the attempt to be definitive about exactly what it is, what factors determine whether something can or cannot be called creative. There are arguments that the product one might create is more important than the process one goes through to create it, and vice versa. There are arguments that inherited personality traits are the determining factors as to whether or not a person can be judged creative, while others say that one's environment provides his or her ability to create.

Within each—product, process, personality, and environment—there are discrepancies of definitions. Some say, for example, that a creative product must be a tangible item; others insist that simple expression of a creative thought can also be called a creative product. Some maintain that the process one goes through in creating is the same for all people, while others think there are as many creative processes as there are individuals. With respect to personality traits, some insist creative people are born, not made; others feel strongly that creative thinking can be taught. Advocates of environmental factors that nurture creative behavior are strong in their beliefs; their adversaries feel the creative person will perfrom regardless of the environment he or she is placed in.

In actuality, any of the above positions can be defended or disputed depending upon what one chooses to prove or disprove. Because teachers are aware of the vast differences among those in their charge, it is advisable to take an eclectic approach, pulling out all the stops, so to speak, in the attempt to develop creative potential in students. The researchers in each of the above areas have taught us a great deal. And as teachers we have learned to employ a wide variety of means to reach students. If standing on one's head and spitting jellybeans is the only way to get to some student, a teacher probably wouldn't be above trying it.

It is important to have a speaking acquaintance, at least, with the issues involved in judging what is or isn't considered creativity. What is discussed here merely skims the surface. Deeper investigation is urged as you try this field of creative behavior on for size. This initial exposure, however, calls for some decisions on your part.

Where end product is concerned, for instance, how will you judge whether or not it is creative? There are two opposing schools of thought. One says that if it is new to the person who has produced it, it is creative. That in spite of the fact that the product has existed before, having been created by someone else or by numerous others, it is new to this individual at this time in his or her life and therefore is a creative product. The opposing school maintains that in order for an end product to be considered creative, it must not have existed before and it must meet particular criteria, criteria that will set it apart from anything that has been produced previously. Some of those criteria are novelty or unusualness, appropriateness to the context in which it is placed, transformation of materials or ideas that overcome conventional constraints. Another thought to keep in mind is that end products can vary greatly as to intent. Two extremes, for example, are products intended to serve a functional purpose and those that are aesthetic expressions. One's own values come into play. Is a new surgical instrument more valuable than a great musical composition?

Judgment of end products raises many questions. Of major importance is the decision you make as a teacher as to whether your students will be judged against themselves and their previous productivity, or whether the norms of society are to be applied in evaluating the worth of their efforts.

In the introduction to his book *The Creative Process*, Brewster Ghiselin states

> *The creative process is the process of change, of development, of evolution, in the organization of subjective life. The inventive minds through whose activity that evolution has been initiated and in large part accomplished have usually been the only ones much concerned with it. Their efforts have rarely been sustained by society, and have sometimes even been hindered.* [1]

Questions about creative process never fail to be interesting and controversial. Some like to attach a mystique to it: It happens, and, all of a sudden, a creative product takes form. How one arrived at the end product is not important; the fact that it exists is what matters. Strong advocates of this view feel it is an abomination or a sacrilege to attempt to analyze the process of getting there.

Those who subscribe to analytical creativity, however, feel that knowledge of the creative behaviors within the process of creating an end product is vital to future productivity. Ghiselin proclaims that "insight into the processes of invention can increase the efficiency of almost any developed and active intelligence." [2]

In recent years, more and more attention has been given to the way the human mind operates. We have acquired knowledge about learning styles and the capacity of the mind that

[1] New York; Mentor Books, 1955, p.12.
[2] Ibid., p.11.

should and will revolutionize educational practices. J. P. Guilford's recent book, *Way Beyond the I.Q.*, is a marvelous contribution to our knowledge of human intelligence.

In addition to the controversy that was mentioned earlier, that is, the individuality or the commonality of creative processes, there is the one that argues whether or not creative processes can be taught. Certainly we can acknowledge those elements of the creative process that have been identified through the study of people who have been judged creative by societal norms or by the creators themselves. We can use that information to identify within ourselves those knowledges, skills, and attitudes toward developing our own potentials, adopting what seems to fit and disregarding what doesn't seem to fit.

Another question that arises is what puts a creative process, when it does occur, into motion? What parts are played by such things as impulse, instinct, inspiration, motivation, stimulation? Should one sit back and wait for a creative process to begin, or are there times when they might be induced? A laugh I've often had on myself is a paper I began in college and never finished called "Moments of Inspiration and What Happens to Them."

Numerous studies have been conducted on personality traits that tend to help or hinder creative output. Among those traits most commonly identified as helpful toward one's creative productivity are

> openness to experience
> independence
> self-confidence
> willingness to risk
> sense of humor or
>   playfulness
> enjoyment of
>   experimentation
> sensitivity
> lack of a feeling of being
>   threatened
> personal courage

unconventionality
flexibility
preference for complexity
goal orientation
internal control
originality
self-reliance
persistence
curiosity
vision
self-assertion
acceptance of disorder
tolerance for ambiguity
motivation
inclination to the off-beat

Personality traits that have been identified as character-
izing creative individuals are often thought of in the light of
Thoreau's person who hears a different drummer. The person
is generally a nonconformist but not necessarily in an abrasive
way. In fact, timidity is often a trait attributed to a creative person. A number of the characteristics seem to be juxtaposed to
others. Are these traits innate, or are they acquired? If they can
be acquired, the question for educators, then, is how can these
traits be developed?

That question leads directly to the influence of one's environment on his or her ability to perform creatively. Most often
we think of the environment that will nurture creative behavior
as one that is supportive of the individual. Support here is not
false praise, but rather honest support that dignifies the individual. Environmental support allows mistakes and encourages
experimentation, openness, and risk taking. It provides a climate for one to explore his or her potential.

Is it always the warm nest, though, that evokes creative
behavior? In initial exposure, perhaps it is. But extreme human
suffering, which necessitates the need for expression into a
creative product, is often grist for the mill for later on. Some of
the world's greatest literature evolved in times of human crisis.
And the saying "Necessity is the mother of invention" is not

trite. Human beings respond to their environments, either actively or passively. Active response is more likely for one who has had an opportunity to develop a sense of self-worth through a supportive environment, particularly in the formative years.

I have sought in this chapter to introduce a variety of ways in which creativity is viewed. Educators find different views useful at different times.

three

Setting the Climate for Creative Behavior

A climate that is conducive to evoking creative behavior can be established in a number of ways, and they are based upon principles of creative behavior that research has confirmed. Climate, or atmosphere, takes into consideration three major factors: the physical, the mental, and the emotional. Knowing what we do about individual styles of learning and the variety of ways a teacher employs motivational strategies to reach different kinds of students, it is desirable to account for all three of the major factors. We also know that the same motivational strategy will not work over and over again for any individual student or whole class.

In giving attention to physical, mental, and emotional aspects of climate, we set a stage for both intended and unintended learning (or motivation toward learning) to occur. In other words, we are providing the conditions for both deliberate and serendipitous types of productivity.

It seems appropriate—no, important—to mention at this point a gross misconception in regard to nurturing creative behavior. Just as John Dewey's Progressive Education Movement was misinterpreted by many and therefore implemented with limited success and sometimes disastrous results, so have some attempts in introducing creative behavior in school curricula met with less than educationally spectacular outcomes. Creativity in the classroom does not mean chaotic conditions that allow students total freedom to express themselves. Nor does it imply the abdication of the role of the teacher as the person in charge. A teacher can never relinquish that primary responsibility for the physical and psychological safety of students. Setting a climate for productivity does not mean creating a totally unstructured, anything-goes condition. In reality, creative productivity imposes upon the individual a good deal of self-discipline and is most effective when the individual is provided with sufficient structure to feel basically secure. People are more willing to risk if they know their whole foundation won't be obliterated as a possible consequence.

THE PHYSICAL CLIMATE

The classroom requires a physical arrangement that is supportive to the kinds of activities the teacher wants to conduct or allow. It need not be elaboratively or expensively equipped. Virtually any existing classroom can be arranged to allow large group and small group spaces, as well as areas for students to work in pairs or alone. If dividers or bookshelves aren't available, one can use such things as cardboard cartons, old curtains, or if materials are really scarce, train the students to imagine dividers. The point is, the teacher needs to provide a setting that affords the kinds of spaces appropriate to different kinds of pursuits. If students can't work alone in an assigned carrel, then they need to have some sort of space that has been allocated to them alone, at least for a given period of time. It could be a portion of a table, a pillow on the floor, a traditional desk facing a window—any spot they can claim as their own.

Just as students are allotted a space of their own, so they should have a secure place to keep the material they are working on. The "keeping place" for their private property can be any sort of container: a shoe box, a compartment in a cabinet, a large envelope, a file folder, a desk. In developing a climate for creativity, the teacher stresses the importance of everyone's respecting the individual's private spaces and properties. In many school situations, everything that students are or produce are on public display: test marks, composition grades, art work, the reading group they are assigned to, their name on the cut list for an athletic team or music group, the remedial math teacher's schedule, the detention list, the psychologist's appointment calendar. If, in creative behavior, we are asking students to take risks, to try new things, to dare to be different, then we need to guarantee them some privacy while they are in the process of risking. Too often we have a tendency to intervene earlier than we should while a student is working something out. We are too quick to point out what is wrong, what improvements could be made, or give helpful hints to speed up the progress. Those early interventions often discourage rather than encourage. The student's physical private place helps build the emotional support crucial to creative productivity.

Other physical-climate factors in the classroom include areas to display students' work: cork boards, tables, shelves, orange crates—anything that can be contrived to give prominence to their creations. Resource materials need to be within reach: scrap paper, newsprint, tape, glue, pencils, markers, scissors as well as books, maps, atlases, encyclopedias and other library-type resources, games, and puzzles. Whether the school is highly endowed financially or not, most teachers manage to equip their classrooms with a variety of manipulatives. Their availability to students at crucial moments plays an important role in encouraging creative behavior.

THE MENTAL CLIMATE

Learning occurs when an individual connects with a stimulus, animate or inanimate, subjectively or objectively, serendipitously or deliberately, thus creating meaning for the learner. Because of the diversity of learning styles and interests among students within a given classroom, the teacher needs to provide a variety of stimuli to account for the differences in what individual students will respond to.

A desirable mental climate is one that challenges but does not overwhelm. In fact, early challenges presented to a student or class should have built-in success for the student. It is through meeting success that one is encouraged to go on. Challenges should then become developmentally more difficult as progress is made.

For the student whose learning style is verbal in orientation, word games that are relatively easy to handle are good to begin with. The Word Ladder provides a good beginning.

Change HATE to LOVE by
changing only one letter at a time.

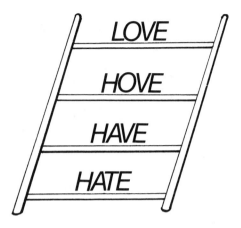

With this or any other type of puzzle or challenge, invite students to create their own. Provide opportunities for students to present their creations to other students either verbally or on a display space. In that way, students themselves keep a particular kind of stimulus going.

Visually oriented students are attracted to "Droodles," which serve as good initial exercises.

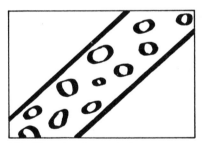

Giraffe going by a window.

They love to figure these out and they love to make them up. This type of student also derives satisfaction from pictorially representing words, such as

WIGGLE

Math fans are attracted to puzzles involving numbers. A simple beginning is, "Can you make eight 8's equal 1,000?"

$$
\begin{array}{r}
8 \\
8 \\
8 \\
88 \\
888 \\
\hline
1,000
\end{array}
$$

More advanced math students will take to problems of greater complexity that require not only a knowledge of mathematics but also flexibility of thinking as well.

Find the missing number.

5	6	7	8	9
52	63	94		18

(The missing number is 46. The bottom row of numbers are the squares—reversed—of the top-row numbers.)

Building associative powers (mentioned in an earlier chapter) helps students meet mental challenges. Developing fluency through such techniques as brainstorming gives students a more positive sense of their mental abilities. Flexibility is inherent in all of the above exercises. Flexibility increases one's options, so that risk taking becomes more commonplace among students, and increasingly difficult challenges are met with a sense of excitement rather than fear or dread.

THE EMOTIONAL CLIMATE

Providing all the appropriate ingredients for physical and mental climates will serve little if the emotional atmosphere is not one that is supportive. A supportive emotional climate affords students the personal security to respond to the physical and mental stimuli that their teacher or their peers have placed before them. It is the security they feel that the established ground rules will not be violated. The ground rules are personal guarantees that allow students to grow at their own rate, retain the privacy of their work until they are ready to share it, and prize their possible differences.

Regardless of the age of the students a teacher might be working with, an atmosphere of trust must be established and maintained. Trust is an elusive concept. It can't be injected like a vaccine and expected to be effective for a given period of time. It requires constant demonstration and reinforcement. Especially in the initial stages of establishing a climate for creative behavior does the teacher need to be the role model for and the gatekeeper of an atmosphere of trust. We have all experienced the feeling of "being burned" and never again risking in certain situations. Violations of trust, particularly with youngsters, can be the most detrimental factors toward one's efforts to evoke creative behavior.

Students need to be kept informed, at all times, of what the classroom agenda is for any given time. Each day, by verbal announcement or written notice, information on the day's goals helps the student to feel secure. That is one way of providing a structure for an environment that is fundamentally safe enough for the student to rise to some personal challenge. All that are needed are simple announcements such as, "Today is quiet, individual work time" or "Today in your small groups we will brainstorm." Students will know whether it is to be a "divergent" or a "convergent" day. If, for example, it is a "divergent" day, then the prevailing ground rules will encourage total openness. Nothing they offer will be regarded as too silly, too far out, impossible, or dumb. There will be no right or wrong, no one will be allowed to criticize or ridicule, and all responses will be accepted. The teacher might like to use a green light to signify such times. A red light, or "convergent" day, means to the student that judgment is to be applied, not harsh, cruel judgment, but selectivity through establishing meaningfull criteria.

Honest support is extremely crucial. Kids are sharper than a lot of adults in recognizing falseness. Praising a student's work that he or she knows is a mess is not supportive and creates mistrust. How one offers criticism is the important thing. Criticism that implies that the *person* isn't worthwile is completely in error. Criticism that states that a *product* isn't worthy of the person's usual performance or potential ability will not be destructive. A gentle way of presenting negative criticism of a product is through self-validation. As an illustration, Louise hands in an original story that is not cohesive and looks sloppy. An ensuing dialogue might go something like this:

TEACHER: Louise, did you get good grades in penmanship and spelling last marking period?

LOUISE: Yes.

TEACHER: Did I hear correctly that you got a raise in your allowance for taking such good care of your little brother?

LOUISE: Yes.

TEACHER: Are you a good skier?

LOUISE: Yes.

TEACHER: Do you have a lot of friends?

LOUISE: Yes.

TEACHER: You do many things well and are well liked. One thing that needs shaping up is this story you've handed in. Did you do a less than acceptable job here?

LOUISE: Yes.

The emotional climate of a classroom toward evoking creative behavior must provide the conditions for students to experience a sense of self-worth, a sense of belonging, and a sense of personal power. They gain a feeling of personal dignity and gain a respect for the dignity of others. The support the students receive is honest, and they learn to be supportive of others. Challenges they are given are developmentally sequenced so that self-confidence is realized.

four

The Individual Student

George T. L. Ainsworth-Land's major work in Transformational Theory provides a framework for observing and assessing the growth and development of an individual student. Indeed, his model has universal applicability, and his book *Grow or Die: The Unifying Principle of Transformation* is worth in-depth investigation. This application just touches on the rudiments of the theory that, in this use of it, provides a map for charting an individual student's progress.

The developmental stages that Land has identified as existing in all living things are

- o Formative
- o Normative
- o Integrative
- o Transformational

In the process of growth and development, a living thing over a period of time strives to maintain more order than disorder. Advancement from one stage of development to the next occurs when the preceding stage no longer provides a nourishing or needed environment. On the human level, this cycle of growth can be viewed from the point of view of a human being's entire lifetime or in the myriad of diversified encounters of growth one experiences throughout a lifetime. In other words, within the major life cycle of an individual are many other developmental cycles, which are dependent upon the innumerable exposures to encounters that offer opportunities for growth. Introducing individuals to the creative potential within themselves requires yet another cycle of growth to be assimilated into a life-style. This particular growth cycle can have enormous impact, affecting simultaneously any number of other cycles in various stages of development.

The beauty of Land's model is not only the awareness one can gain of what is happening within oneself at any given time, but also the reassurance that whatever stage one might be experiencing is quite normal and necessary. In some of my work I have based the student-teaching experience on the Transformational Theory model. Over and over again, interns expressed the comfort they derived from understanding the naturalness of each stage of development, even the most difficult stages. Briefly, and with my interpretations, the stage can be defined this way:

1. *Formative stage:*   The need to control a new environment, to get one's feet on the ground. An egocentric stage in which the self must learn to feel secure, learning the ground rules for this new environment, establishing one's presence, identity of self, certainty of one's own existence in the environment.

2. *Normative stage:*   The newly established self seeks likeness to that self, is influenced by others who share samenesses, becomes

"one of the gang," does not want to be thought of as different, feels a need to replicate appearances and behaviors he or she observes, requires a sense of belonging, may experience self-consciousness through fear of appearing different from others.

3. *Integrative stage:* Being just like everyone else is no longer appealing. The ritualism of sameness in appearance and behavior becomes boring and no longer useful. One begins to appreciate what is different within oneself and the differentnesses of others. Desire to share differentness, thereby enriching one's own environment and contributing to the enrichment of others' environments. Feeling of pride in one's own uniqueness. More confidence in a more finely defined self.

4. *Transformational stage:* The opportunities for enrichment through sharing of self with others has stagnated. The level of sharing has remained on a plane that offers no more opportunity for growth. One recognizes that in order to continue to grow, one must move on. One feels the need for a major change in one's life and/or life-style. Definitely a crisis time because it means a letting go of what has been pleasing and secure. One realizes possible trauma that could occur, fearful of the personal risk involved, the existential leap into uncertainty. One can either slip back or forge ahead. Slipping back means not making any waves and staying comfortable; forging ahead means the

beginning of another cycle and new
struggles for identity and personal
space, literally a transformation.

Consider what a human life over a span of years would
look like in terms of the Ainsworth-Land model. The formative
years of human growth and development are infancy, early
childhood, and primary school years. A baby announces its
presence and makes its demands upon others. The role is one of
dependency, but is by no means passive. Between the ages of
two and, say, seven children are further establishing themselves
by claiming rights, toys, space, parents, and so on. They are
gaining physical coordination, speech, mental acuity, and are
experimenting with a variety of emotions. Toward the end of
those years children begin testing their independence from the
adults in their lives, and they waver back and forth between de-
pendence and independence.

The wavering is characteristic of children's attempts to
move into the next stage of development, the normative stage.
Having established their ground as members of the human
race, children branch out from the adults upon whom they have
been dependent as they enter preadolescence and adolescence.
The normative stage of development is the one in which influence is the name of the game. The youngster has discovered he
or she has peers and wants to be just like them. "Mom, I'll just
die if I can't have this kind of sneakers!" Or that kind of
haircut, bike, or tennis lessons. The adults from the former
stage don't know anything anymore. The kid down the street,
the latest youthful rock star, the teen magazines are now the
authorities. Peer group pressure at this age level seems to be an
attempt at cloning. If in the crowd an adolescent considers it
cool to smoke, the adolescent will smoke. If it's cool to do
homework and get good grades, he or she will do that. Each
group has its own set of cools and taboos. The adolescent has
such a strong need to belong that he or she will go along with
whatever are the accepted behaviors among the group members.

As individuals progress into early adulthood and adulthood, they grow tired of being identified as one of the crowd

and bored with the sameness of appearances and behaviors, and they begin to like what is different about themselves and what is different in others. The desire to share differences instead of samenesses all the time signals the beginning of the integrative stage. Such individuals want to integrate more kinds of things and people into their lives. Discovering their own uniqueness and being able to share that uniqueness is important. Such people are defining their individuality and want to exercise their own creativity and enjoy a sense of mutuality with others. It is a period of sharing both pleasures and pains. It is the acquisition of a knowledge of oneself as both a giver and a receiver. As long as the environment continues to be nourishing, the individual is content to remain in the integrative stage. The recognition of growth through mutual sharing is a very satisfying place to be.

When, however, people find that the integrative environment is no longer able to sustain their own growth and creativity, they experience a need to leave it. The pull to stay can be very strong, for it has seemed close to being utopian. Considerable pain accompanies the decision to leave or to stay. Attempts are made to re-create the excitement that that particular environment once held. But replication of anything is really characteristic of the normative stage, and the adult recognizes the futility of this. Transformation means having the willingness and the will to make a sometimes dramatic change in one's life. It requires seeking a new environment that will nourish and sustain continued growth and development. It is the risk of beginning a cycle all over again, of establishing oneself, of belonging, of integrating, and perhaps, of again transforming.

Because of the heaviness of looking at Transformational Theory as it might apply to an entire human life-span, a recapitulation of the stages is now offered through something a bit lighter—learning to play the piano.

1. *Formative stage:*   learning the keyboard, learning the notes, coordinating your fingers, gaining control.

2. *Normative stage:*   trying to make the music sound like music you've heard before, hoping

	people will recognize the songs and pieces you play, copying the style of playing of a pianist you admire.
3. *Integrative stage:*	gaining enough confidence to integrate a style of your own with the printed music, trying to interpret the composer, sensing a mutuality with the composer and his or her music.
4. *Transformational stage:*	composing your own music, rearranging existing music, taking up another instrument, beginning a new cycle of growth.

The students in your classroom will be experiencing similar stages of development as you work toward evoking creative behavior. It is well to remember that several cycles of development can be occurring at the same time within an individual. In a teacher's striving toward helping a student move from dependency to greater independence in the area of creative behavior, the stage of another cycle of growth happening simultaneously can serve either to hinder or to enhance the cycle having to do with creative potential. And, conversely, the creativity cycle will influence other cycles. In addition, as teachers well know, stages of any kinds of development vary considerably among groups of students who are the same age. Teachers are attuned to individual differences and recognize states of readiness necessary for a student to advance to later levels.

A very important facet of teaching to evoke creative behavior is awareness of a student's stage of development and his or her degree of readiness to advance to a subsequent stage. The growth cycle described in Transformational Theory assumes that a "normal" individual will remain in a particular stage for as long as is necessary. Individuals move on to the next stage when the present one no longer serves their needs. When that environment is used up, so to speak, they seek a new level of nourishment. It's like a houseplant that needs transplanting into a larger pot because it has outgrown its environment.

In guiding students toward developing their creative potential, being able to assess where they are in the stages of development and when readiness for a subsequent stage occurs are very useful teacher skills. The Transformational Theory model provides a framework that facilitates the process. Observations of the student's behavior reveal characteristics of each stage of development. Observable behaviors—the student's work, relationships with others, attitudes—can be noted on an assessment sheet just as you would do for any other type of assessment. In a separate Creative Behavior looseleaf notebook, have a separate page for each student's progress that might look like this:

	Creative Behavior Observations			
Student				
Date	Formative Behaviors	Normative Behaviors	Integrative Behaviors	Transformational Behaviors

Using the characteristics for each stage of growth given earlier in this chapter, make entries in the appropriate columns and date each entry. It is simple to chart forward progress and regression by noting sequential dates of observations in the left-hand column and writing observation notes opposite the date they were entered.

Because exploring one's creative potential involves considerable personal risk, more for some people than for others, a reluctance to leave a comfortable and secure stage might be more prevalent in this type of growth and development than it is in other types. For instance, a student might feel very secure being involved in group brainstorming but quite fearful of striking out on his or her own ideational efforts. This student appears to be comfortable in activities of the second stage and exhibits reluctance to move to the third stage. Too much nudging by the teacher could be very threatening and perhaps detrimental. Careful planning, however, on the teacher's part always to alternate between individual and group kinds of activities that students are taking part in will help the student gain confidence in his or her own abilities.

One of the most difficult transitions is between the second and third stages. Teacher strategy needs to include a constant reinforcement of diversity, illustrating that the strength of civilization rests with the singular contributions of many people and that individual talents developed and shared are most important. Especially among students who are socially in the formative stage of development, when peer influence is very strong, it is crucial to reinforce individual contributions in terms of creative behavior. Kept in the context of creative behavior, the teacher is less likely to tread on dangerous ground with students' social development since students are receptive to social influences of peers and do not welcome adult intervention.

From another perspective, think of the student who at this time would like to demonstrate some differentnesses but the social climate among his or her peers is not a tolerable one for such behavior. By the teacher's setting a tone within the group for acceptance of individuality and praise for singular efforts, the student is encouraged to risk his or her differentness. The teacher's sensitivity is essential to this delicate balance.

In spite of the fact that the teacher may establish a climate conducive to creative behavior, encourage diversity, and develop strategies to balance individual and group activities, an individual student may continue to exhibit first- or second-stage behavior for what seems to be too long a period of time. For one thing, don't worry about it. When the stage that students are in fails to serve their needs, they will advance. When whatever it is they seem to be accomplishing by staying put is no longer fulfilling, they will move forward. For another thing, it is quite possible that the student is taking the risks of moving to the next stage privately. Students will work privately sometimes so that possible failures may also be kept secret. You may not find out about the failures, but you'll be certain to hear about the successes.

Time should somehow be set aside for individual conferences with students. Singluar attention for each student is very reinforcing for the student and very revealing for the teacher. Conferences should never be times when pressure is exerted. Rather, they should be quiet talks about the student's work, feelings, interests, and so on. In no way should the student interpret the conference as evaluative. This is not to say that evaluation is disregarded; it isn't. This private conference is just not the time for it.

Before sitting down with a student, the teacher should do some homework on what the student has been doing. The conference will yield much greater results if the teacher doesn't have to shuffle through papers or continue to ask the student such things as, "What is it you've been working on?" Those kinds of things say to the student that the teacher is just going through some routine and isn't really interested in me and what I'm doing.

The conference should not appear to be, nor should it be, routine. The context of it will and should vary as much as individual students vary. Honing in on where students are in terms of their own growth and development is the key to how the teacher conducts the conference. For example, students who are still very much in the formative steps of development are looking for controls in their environment. If some students' personal security requires control of their situation, they might be asking, very legitimately in terms of where they are at this time, for controls from this adult in their life. If that's how you, as the teacher, read their needs, then go ahead and provide the controls. If students ask, "What should I do next?," tell them. Depending upon the student and how well you have diagnosed the situation, a kind of weaning can be attempted, but not forced. Having done your homework on the students and really hearing where they are coming from during the conference will guide you in what to do.

For the purpose of diagnosing stage development in creative behavior, let us take a hypothetical student, Pat, as the example. Pat is a bright young girl, who gets good grades and is well mannered and popular. She is excited about learning to develop her creative potential.

1. *Formative stage:*   The activities the teacher is providing are fun, but Pat finds it hard to defer judgment. She's used to evaluating her own efforts because she has always been a high achiever, evidenced by her report card. She knows that divergent thinking provides many alternatives to the way she might approach things, but she is the kind of person who likes rapid closure on the "right" answers. It is frustrating for her to "stay loose" for too long a period of time. She is determined, however, to gain control of this skill of divergence.

2. *Normative stage:*   Pat has always been the norm, the standard that has influenced her peers, both academically and socially. She has felt a great deal of responsibility in living up to the expectations others have had of her. It is difficult for her to witness in this creative behavior class that others—less bright, less popular—are beginning to influence her classmates because they've caught on to techniques such as deferring judgment. She isn't jealous, really, just uneasy. Her friends urge her to let loose and be a little crazy in group brainstorming sessions. She eventually tries, and her friends cheer her on.

3. *Integrative stage:*   Pat is experiencing a lot of joy in sharing the outcomes of her work

with others and is appreciating what others are producing, even though there is a big difference among the kinds of things being done. She's writing poetry in free verse, which she has never done before, and likes to read it to the class. She has learned a great deal from a friend who is designing a new car, another who is writing plays, and another who has invented a mechanical part.

4. *Transformational stage:*

With all the new exposure she has been experiencing and the satisfaction she is enjoying through this new way of relating with her classmates, Pat keeps thinking about different things she might like to do with her life. It's early yet, but there seem to be a lot more doors open. "And so what if I make a few mistakes," she says to herself. In the meantime, she'll try her hand at several different things.

Pat is obviously a student who has been quite rigid in a role set by expectations of self and others. Her behavior provides clues for the teacher to guide her in developing her creative potential. Not with all students but certainly with this one, as with most, the teacher can help Pat look at her own development by explaining the stages of growth. The student's learning that each stage is normal and quite necessary will make her next growth cycle much easier to deal with. Self-understanding of the ways in which one grows and develops facilitates the learning process. Many people's growth suffers because they have no knowledge of what is happening to them. The mystique causes anxiety and self-doubt, real cripplers to growth and development.

Students can use their knowledge of the stages of development as benchmarks so long as they understand the necessity of completing their growth within any given stage before moving ahead and that is okay. The old gold-star method of recognition for advancing to the next level is totally inappropriate. Competition among students in that way defeats the purpose. A healthy atmosphere in which a student can honestly say, "I'm not ready for that yet" or "I want to do some work in this area first" and have it accepted, is what the teacher should stive for. Naturally, age levels and specific situations have to be taken into account; and only you, the teacher, can make the kinds of judgments appropriate to your own students.

INDIVIDUAL PROJECTS

The number of individual projects a teacher might expect students to carry out is determined by the length of time that can be devoted to activities in creative behavior. Individual types of work, however, can be done both within class periods and outside. Complexity of projects is determined by the age level of the students as well as time. Nevertheless, try not to underestimate the capacities of students at any age level to be able to handle rather complex topics, especially when you are dealing with the developing creative potential. As students gain confidence in their abilities through exposure to this area of learning, they tend to tackle topics that seem quite complex for them, at least in the eyes of the adults working with them.

Two kinds of projects are described here. "Fun-with-a-purpose projects" are whole-class assignments although one of the intents is to encourage individuality. "Major individual projects" are determined in terms of subject matter by the individual, but follow a problem-solving process.

Fun-with-a-Purpose Projects

These project assignments are designed to challenge the imagination, to provide activities that require, for the most part, manual as well as mental effort, and to provide activities that are fun and produce more immediate and tangible results.

1. Totem Pole A totem pole is the traditional expression of the individual. The end product should have meaning for the individual. The totem pole can actually be constructed, can be designed, or can be written about. Although some students may choose to have the totem pole represent themselves over their life-spans to date, it is suggested that they limit the expression to some facet of their present lives that is important to them or to one present emotion they are experiencing.

Usually the products express some present interest or emotion. A junior high school boy who has just gotten into serious card playing nailed an upright board to a base and tacked a deck of cards onto it to illustrate different poker hands. He called it "The Hierarchy of Poker." Another young man, who was having trouble with the music teacher, reproduced the music teacher's picture several times. He tacked the pictures, one above the other, onto a three-foot-high pole and called his creation "Ego." A girl used hard-boiled eggs to depict some courageous and tough women in history.

The totem pole assignment is one that is invaluable to the teacher. Through them, students have an open opportunity to express themselves, and the self-revealing products provide a great deal of information for the teacher. So, while the assignment is fun, it accomplishes purposes on both sides. "Show and Tell" on the day the assignment is due provides an experience in mutual sharing (integrative stage) that can set a healthy tone in the classroom, the benefits of which can be reaped for a long time afterward.

2. Original Greeting Cards This assignment can be done during a class period when things need a lift. The final products can be greeting cards for existing celebrated occasions or occasions the students make up. They can be general or for a specific person, so long as the message is not a hurting one. The only materials the teacher provides are construction paper, crayons, and scissors. Students may use anything else they have with them to enhance their creations. Again, show-and-tell at the end of the period.

3. Ingredients Projects   Ingredients projects are best accomplished as home assignments because of the materials needed. Following are two examples:

An ingredients project asks students to take five ingredients and put them together in a way that they think no one else will put them together. The first project includes as materials such things as newspaper, candles, pins, tape, and rubber bands. Whatever materials you choose to assign, be sure some of them are highly flexible, but don't mention this factor to the students. Pins, for example, are a highly flexible ingredient and challenge the imagination. Pins can be straight pins, safety pins, clothes pins, bowling pins, jewelry, and so forth. Candles also offer flexibility. They come in all sizes and shapes; they can be left whole or melted. At least one ingredient has to be something that can hold other things together such as tape, rubber bands, glue, paper clips, chewing gum, and so on.

The day ingredients projects are brought in becomes an event. For the most part, students take great pride in their creations and are eager to share their interpretations of the ingredients. It's an atmosphere of friendly competition and mutual appreciation. These projects, as well as the totem poles, deserve display space. This might be a good time to make friends with the custodian. Invite him or her in for Show and Tell.

The second ingredients project allows greater latitude in materials that are used and calls for greater use of the imagination. The ingredients might be cardboard, string, something metal, something green, and one "free" ingredient. You might want to enhance the activity by asking that the final product have a specific meaning behind it that the student can write or tell about.

The ingredients project is a fun activity, but it also teaches skills of creative behavior, fluency, flexibility, originality, elaboration, and associative powers. Although it isn't stressed, students are not only applying these skills, they are also utilizing a problem-solving process. If it is appropriate for your setting, students might do a postanalysis of how they used the skills they've already learned. Or they might analyze how they went about achieving the end product through a problem-solving methodology. It's a good opportunity to illustrate how they are, consciously or otherwise, applying a process.

4. Invention　Students are asked to come up with a totally new invention or to improve upon something that already exists. This activity exercises all of the skills just mentioned and is valuable in developing sensitivity to needs and problems. As in the totem pole assignment, a design for the end product is sufficient, since actual construction may be impracticable or impossible. Students will, however, often construct models.

Some students will produce working mechanical gadgets. Other students, whose inclinations take them in other directions, have produced such things as

- unusual mixed media in the visual arts—a highly effective use of sand on an oil painting
- a dictionary of devices useful to poets—in this instance, an onomatopoeia listing for several verbs
- morphological charts to assign home chores fairly
- a musical composition using instruments not usually combined
- artwork derived from physics experiments—in this case, pendulums swinging with different-colored pencils attached.
- a creative guide to practicing the piano

A business-minded student invented a packaging device. Two aspirins were sealed in a package that opened up into a paper cup, for travel purposes. Another invented and constructed a new board game using an eight-sided die. Another designed and constructed a piece of clothing for travel that, with a few minor adjustments, could serve as formal wear, play clothes, work clothes, and weather-protective clothes. All of these students, and others, sought patents.

Teachers must, of course, exercise their judgment as to how many of and in what depth the preceding fun-with-a-purpose projects are appropriate for their students. Any of the projects can be modified to suit specific situations. Others can be invented that might be more appropriate. The value of these projects for the individual student is high. And their value in climate setting is high. Through these kinds of activities, student creative productivity is greatly increased, and positive self-concept takes a sharp turn upward.

MAJOR INDIVIDUAL PROJECTS

Students provide the subject matter for major individual projects according to their own interests. The selection of topics for projects should be carefully guided—but by no means dictated—by the teacher. That the project is truly worthwhile for and of interest to the student is what is important. Whatever the students choose to work on, as well as the results they achieve should represent a meaningful experience for them. Therefore, considerable time and effort should be expended in helping students select a topic. A topic that is too broad or too shallow can result in frustration or boredom. Not only should the topics interest the students but they should also challenge them.

For the students who are certain of what they would like to pursue as an individual project and for the ones who haven't the faintest idea what they would like to do, a greater insight into their own aims and/or values can be gained by some preliminary goal setting or by attempting to answer some probing questions. For the first individual project, merely asking students to set ten goals they would like to achieve within a specified time period serves the purpose. Rank ordering the goals, either before or during a conference with the teacher, helps them make the selection. Because the first major project comes early in the student's exposure to creative behavior, topics should not involve as great a depth as a second project might. The first time through, using a problem-solving methodology on a topic a student is close to should just about guarantee success at the outset. It should challenge but be attainable.

From the second major project, however, the teacher should expect greater depth. By this time the student is familiar with procedures and has gained enough self-confidence to attempt something more difficult. Throughout, there has been an emphasis on self-knowledge and awareness of one's own growth and development. Asking students to respond in writing to some probing questions about themselves might be appropriate. Be certain to assure them that the responses are for their eyes alone and no one else's. Sidney J. Parnes has developed a series of questions that are excellent for this purpose. Students who are not sure what they would like to pursue are forced to do some concrete thinking; students who have a pursuit in mind benefit from thinking in depth. Parnes calls his questions "The Mess." They offer a good way of getting at problems, needs, desires, and opportunities for problem solving with an eye toward focusing on a project topic.

1. What would you like to do, have, accomplish?
2. What do you wish would happen?
3. What would you like to do better?
4. What do you wish you had more time or money for?
5. What more would you like to get out of life?
6. What are your unfulfilled ambitions?
7. What angered you recently?
8. What makes you tense, anxious?
9. What have you complained about?
10. What misunderstandings did you have?
11. With whom would you like to get along better?
12. What changes for the worse are you aware of in attitudes of others?
13. What would you like to get others to do?
14. What changes will you have to introduce?
15. What takes too long?
16. What is wasted?
17. What is too complicated?
18. What "bottlenecks" exist?

19. In what ways are you inefficient?
20. What wears you out?
21. What would you like to organize better? [1]

Naturally, your adaptation of "The Mess" should be modified in accord with our own teaching situation. If you use the entire list of questions, perhaps you would like to have students respond to any ten of their choice. Another way to approach the questions is to set an initial time limit of one minute to respond to each question. However you decide in terms of the questions, they are helpful toward focusing on project topics.

Once topics have been selected, students can employ the problem-solving process which is explained in detail in a later chapter. How each student proceeds is determined by what the needs seem to be. Students who have set satisfactory goals or stated a clearly defined problem to be solved can move right along. Students who are struggling for direction might be advised to use the stream-of-consciousness method for becoming more articulate about their concerns. This kind of student will require more hand holding and teacher direction before he or she is able to proceed alone.

Regardless of whether or not the project calls for a tangible end product, written accounts of the students' procedures should be required, for their own benefit as well as the teacher's.

Working through a major individual project for the first time will at times be frustrating and at other times exhilarating, but the benefits to one's entire learning process are enormous.

[1]Parnes, Sidney J. *Creative Behavior Guidebook.* New York: Charles Scribner's Sons, 1967, p. 117.

five

Group Approaches

ABOUT GROUPS

A discussion of group activity in evoking creative behavior needs to be put in perspective in light of the variety of ways in which groups are currently viewed. The idea of groups has been prevalent in our thinking in recent years: in therapy, in counseling, in education, and in the popular adaptations of the Human Potential Movement.

It is the nature of humankind to group ourselves, for any number of reasons, beyond the obvious governmental and other protective levels. We group ourselves to share our commonalities and differences, for purposes of mutual support, to accomplish stated tasks, or simply for social enjoyment. We serve on committees or task forces, we join clubs or teams, we attend neighborhood picnics or coffee klatsches. Regardless of the seriousness of intent that characterizes any group gathering, there is the sharing of commonalities and differences, and mutual support is an available benefit.

"Groupness" took on a life of its own during the late 1960s and early 1970s. Snatches of existing and developing psychological therapies gained enormous popularity. New programs emerged by the dozens proposing individual awareness and fulfillment through the group experience. As with any popular movement that permits a bandwagon approach, the concept of groupness contained among its proponents windfall profiteers who toyed, sometimes quite dangerously, with participants' emotional lives. In addition to weekend or longer programs were the myriad of communities that arose. Some communal-living arrangements are truly beautiful in concept and practice; others have preyed on and taken advantage of those who are lonely and insecure.

The intense interest in groups, however, sparked the revival and/or development in educational programming of important interpersonal skills and concepts. The amount of attention to such things as active listening, feedback, empathetic response, self-validation, and honest support were therapeutic in nature and advanced a psychologically healthy countenance for the participant.

These skills and concepts are contributing factors to the umbrella concept of trust that authentic groups work at maintaining. When a sufficient level of trust exists within a group, the individual experiences a greater sense of personal freedom to be more open, to be willing to risk, to try new things, to take a chance with ideas or behaviors that may not otherwise be brought to light. The natural result is a greater degree of trust in oneself and the development of a more positive self-concept.

The climate of a supportive group also fosters within the individual an open-mindedness toward others. As one feels acceptance of self within the group, so does he or she become more accepting of others and their ideas. The power of a "group think" can be an exhilarating experience. Operating under the deferred-judgment principle of brainstorming, for instance, the members of the group share their spontaneous thinking and spark one another's thoughts. Each individual senses his or her responsibility toward the group's productivity. As momentum builds, the productivity of the group increases, and the individual members experience a surge of power within themselves to be more productive, because among the group members is a reciprocity of openness and acceptance of one another's contributions.

It is on this basis of mutual support and encouragement that a number of types of groups can and do function effectively in a classroom designed to evoke creative behavior. Before discussing possible types of groups and how they might operate, it is important to talk about individuals and how they contribute to a group. For the moment, think of creative ability as being a matter of degree and kind and of creative productivity as a matter of focus. And, of course, the realization of one's true creative ability can be a great distance away from the potential or promise that might be indicated. Also, as we know, an individual can show strength in one type of creative ability and weakness in another. For example, some people are highly fluent and not at all flexible; others might demonstrate associative powers but are unable to be elaborative. In this sense, the nature of one's creative ability dictates the way in which he or she functions toward productivity. The other side of the coin in regard to creative productivity is the focus for one's efforts. Focus is determined by one's life experience, interests, leaning, goals, and so on.

Within any given group of people, there is a wide variety of abilities and usually considerable diversity of foci. What, on the surface, might seem to be conflicting dichotomies, in reality can be the force behind the group's successful functioning. The group becomes an instructor. Members learn through exposure and example to develop their own possible areas of weakness. It's catching, you might say. It is not unusual for a student to say to me, "I learned how to do that from so-and-so when our group was working."

In terms of focus, the group members' exposure to one another helps broaden interests and provide alternatives for goals and directions—all of which enhance divergent behavior. Another important outcome of these group experiences is the heightening of positive human relations through mutual respect of one another's contributions to the process. I'd like to illustrate that point with an example from one of the first high school creativity classes I taught. In one of the small working groups in this class in a midwestern suburb were two students who, under usual circumstance, would not be in a high school class together, nor would they be likely to mix socially. The boy was of the black-jacket, motorcycle variety, and the girl was the blonde cheerleader type. The particular group they were in had been deliberately randomly selected. Once the group had developed and become functional, it became obvious that the boy and girl complemented each other in a very meaningful way. The boy had an uncanny ability in original thinking but lacked the capacity to articulate his thinking. The girl appeared to be too peer influenced to risk original thought but could elaborate upon and refine the boy's ideas. (There is no connection between the types of ability and the sexes of the students.) They became a highly productive team and taught each other a great deal in the process. Their example taught all of us something.

THE POWER OF GROUPS
AND SOME CAUTIONS
ABOUT GROUP IDENTITY

Groups can be powerful forces in either positive or negative ways. The teacher plays a vital role in maintaining the positive forces and being alert to and keeping in check the possible negative forces. As is true in all effective teaching, skillful planning and careful guidance of students' activities will result in group experiences that have positive rather than negative outcomes.

The teacher is responsible for initially establishing the kind of classroom climate that allows and encourages individual students to grow and develop. Group experiences are valued inasmuch as they support the individual's development and demonstrate the positive aspects of individuals working together toward a common goal. In a classroom situation designed to evoke creative behavior, the individual needs to have opportunities to receive psychological support and to be able to provide that kind of support for others. It is analogous to a sports team in which the individual players psych one another up so that each is encouraged to do his or her best. The individual receives a tremendous amount of nourishment from these overt, supportive behaviors and is perhaps able to perform beyond self-expectations. Achievement, as we know, provides even greater inner strength and self-confidence.

Belonging to and being accepted and valued by a group is a normal human need. Indeed, for many people positive group experience is the nourishment that promotes feelings of self-significance. There is a danger in the possibility that an individual will derive feelings of self-worth only when functioning in a group; in that case the relationship to the group is one of dependency, and the person senses an inability to be productive alone. A major consideration the instructor should take into account when planning a class in creative behavior is the careful structuring of activities so that the activities alternate between individual types and shared types. In chapter one a diagram was introduced illustrating the manner in which it was discovered that the highly creative individual behaves.

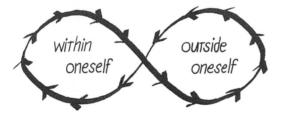

Such individuals seek information outside themselves but also respect themselves as a source. It is crucial that activities are designed to foster this concept. The instructor must have strategies in order that there is always a balance between individual and shared activities. Then, as the class progresses, the teacher needs to remain alert to any individual student who is having difficulty doing independent work because a need for group identity has emerged. Guarding against a student's psychological dependency upon a group is not an easy task for a teacher, but it is a very necessary one.

Along these same lines, it is important that the composition of groups within the classroom does not remain static during the duration of the class. It is far healthier, with respect to what has already been said, for a student to have the opportunity to work within different groupings, allowing him or her a broader range of exposures and relationships.

Preparing students to work in groups might include some exercises in self-awareness that are simple yet help one to gain some insight as to how they relate to others. For instance, the following three short exercises can help determine aggressive/passive patterns of behavior. Wait until all three exercises have been presented before verbally processing any results.

1. Make Waves   Arrange the class in a circle, standing up. Ask them to join hands and pretend that they are an ocean. On a given signal, ask them to "make waves."

2. Volunteers   With the class all sitting down, tell them you need four or five volunteers. Ask the volunteers to come up to the front or into the middle of the group.

Then tell the volunteers to just go back to their seats, that you really didn't want them for anything just now.

3. Picker/Pickee   Tell the class that you want them to pair off for the next exercise. Tell them to look around the room and make sure that the person who becomes a partner is someone with whom they'll feel comfortable talking openly about themselves. (It is best to have a group standing before beginning this exercise so that an individual feels free to move around the room in search of a partner.)

When partners have been determined, ask everyone to sit down.

When the three exercises have been completed, processing can begin. In psychological education programs this activity is defined as the cognitive processing of affective experience. The processing form suggested here is but one of many possible forms.

Remember that the stated purpose for conducting these exercises is to help students determine within themselves possible aggressive/passive patterns of behavior. Ultimately in psychological educational programming, after one has had an opportunity to ascertain patterns of behavior, he or she attempts to determine which patterns seem to be beneficial or detrimental. Here we are talking about one possible behavior pattern with one short sequence of exercises to elicit a degree of self-awareness prior to some group experiences.

Suggested processing for the foregoing activity is a series of questions that you ask students to consider in regard to themselves. Tell them that you want them to think about each question and that they do not have to give an answer out loud. Although you may want to have voluntary sharing of the responses, allow enough silent time for each student to ponder his or her own reactions. With younger children it is necessary to review the exercise first and attend to factual items. In other words, in earlier stages of growth and development, levels of understanding may go only so far as knowing what happened, without students being able to draw any conclusions with respect to behavior patterns. Do not concern yourself with or attempt to force the drawing of conclusions on any one student. Information you, the teacher, gain about individual students as a result of the exercise will be helpful as you set up and guide your groups.

A series of questions about the exercises you might ask them are the following:

1. What happened when you were asked to "make waves?"
2. Did you move both of your arms right away?
3. Did the people on each side of you move your arms before you moved them?
4. Did you like being the one to start the motion, or are you glad someone else started first?
5. When I asked for volunteers, did you volunteer or not volunteer?

6. What went through your mind when I asked for volunteers?

7. I didn't say what you were volunteering for. Did that make a difference in what you decided to do?

8. Do you usually volunteer or not volunteer?

9. When I asked the group to pair up, what did you do?

10. Did you think of someone you feel comfortable talking with?

11. Did you go up to that person?

12. Did someone pick you right away?

13. Did you pick someone right away, or did you wait to be picked?

14. Whenever you're asked to pair up, do you usually pick someone right away, or do you wait until someone else chooses you?

15. Is there anything you learned about yourself in doing these three exercises?

It is obvious that the maturity level of your students needs to be considered in how these exercises are handled or, indeed, whether they are used at all. However, these or similar exercises can provide insight for the teacher about individual student behavior and/or needs in regard to effective grouping. The major question to be considered is whether the group work that occurs seems to be an enhancement or a detriment to the individual's sense of identity. That is what the teacher must be alerted to as groups begin to function. As teachers, we know that peer acceptance is part of a natural stage of growth and development, and we expect a normal amount of attempting to please and wanting to become one of the crowd. It is when being influenced by others seems to have reached extremes that the teacher should take action to alter it.

A role-playing exercise can help students become aware of how effectively a group functions according to roles individuals within the group play.

ROLE-PLAYING EXERCISE

Choose any timely topic for discussion. Have students each take a three-by-five index card and tell them not to reveal its contents to anyone else. Tell them to follow the directions on their cards while taking part in the discussion. Possible role directions for the cards are below. The size of the group will determine the number of them that you need, but make sure that if you use a small number, the selected roles will accomplish the task. Adjust the directions to suit the age level you are working with.

1. Be a questioner. Challenge everything that is said. Ask people to prove what they say.

2. Choose someone in the group to pick on. Even if that person doesn't speak, pick on him or her for not taking part in the discussion.

3. Act bored. Let everyone know that the whole discussion is a waste of your time.

4. Be a subject changer. Keep introducing new topics. Never be willing to discuss what the group is discussing.

5. Be a storyteller. Everything that is mentioned reminds you of a story. Tell the story.

6. Act very tired. Yawn. You try to be interested, but you are just too tired. Finally, just fall asleep.

7. Keep pretending not to understand what is going on. Ask a lot of questions, saying that you just don't understand.

8. Be a clockwatcher. Keep asking people what time it is. Look at your own watch or theirs often. Appear to be anxious for the discussion to end.

9. Be an interrupter. Interrupt almost everyone who speaks.

10. You do not want the group to have any arguments. You try to keep peace and keep everything pleasant.

11. You agree with everything that is said. You agree with one person and then with another, even though they may be saying opposite things.

12. Be determined to win every argument that might arise. Start arguments and try to show everyone else that you are right and they are wrong.

13. Be the expert on every topic that is mentioned. Show the group that you know more about every topic than anyone else does.

14. Be yourself.

The length of the discussion depends upon the age levels represented and how long it takes for most of the roles to become apparent. When the discussion is halted, have each person read his or her card to the rest of the group. This activity is an obvious exaggeration. Subsequent processing should focus around the kinds of individual behavior within a group that prevent the group from progressing. This usually turns out to be a fun activity, but it also raises levels of awareness regarding individual behavior within a group.

TYPES OF FUNCTIONAL GROUPS

Following are descriptions of functional groups the author has found to work effectively in her classes.

Ideational Groups

When a student is working on an individual project and is at a point in the process for which it would be helpful to have a group ideational session, that student requests a group to brainstorm a particular phase of his or her project. The student can request that the group, usually six to eight members, be either heterogenous or homogenous in composition. A heterogenous group would be composed of students whose individual-project foci are fairly unrelated. The benefit of this kind of ideatoinal group is the diversity of associations the members are able to make. A homogenous group, on the other hand, is composed of students whose individual projects are somewhat related in foci. For instance, this group might all be working on projects that are literary. The benefit of this type of group is that its members all share an understanding of the basic task, even though the medium of expression might be quite different, that is, a poet has an understanding of a playwright's task.

Group Projects

Group projects provide the opportunity for students to work together toward a common goal. It is a good kind of activity to alternate with individual efforts. Operating both group and individual activities simultaneously tends to be mutually stimulating and supportive.

Have the class suggest possible topics for group projects and determine actual choices. Group size can be from three to eight in number, or a whole class can elect to work on one major topic, with small groups handling subdivisions of the project. In so far as possible, have each student working on a group project in which he or she is truly interested.

The length of time allotted for the completion of the project is determined by such things as the depth of the content, the attention span of the students, and the manner in which the teacher is assimilating different kinds of classroom work at the time. Pacing in this type of classroom activity is highly important in order to keep the work stimulating and yet not competitive for time with other kinds of work that are occurring simultaneously.

The group decides how individual responsibilities will be divided up, but basically all members are responsible for all phases of the project. For instance, all members have input regarding the problem statement, but two members might do the actual writing of it. It is the teacher's responsibility to see that there is fairness in the allotment of tasks.

The organization of the work can follow a creative problem-solving process. A method of procedure should be available, particularly if it is the first time around for a major endeavor by a group. A suggested sequence might go as follows:

1. Explore the vague problem.
2. Articulate the problem statement.
3. Determine subproblems.
4. Conduct factual research.
5. Employ ideational techniques.
6. Select evaluative criteria.
7. Evaluate.
8. Implement.

The teacher can use various means of checking on the progress of each group: written or oral progress reports, checklists, observations, and so on. Whatever means are employed, in-progress as well as end-product evaluations should be made. In so far as it is possible, the teacher should play a facilitative role rather than a directive one.

GROUPS AROUND CATEGORIES OF INTEREST

Students working on individual projects that fall into a particular category form a group for purposes of mutual support. Some categories might be the following:

1. Literary
2. Visual Arts
3. Sociological
4. Musical
5. Domestic
6. Practical
7. Mechanical
8. Scientific
9. Recreational

A recreational group, for instance, might include a student inventing a new board game, one who is developing a new game involving a basketball, one who is creating unique stuffed toys, and so forth.

An initial, teacher-directed meeting is scheduled during which group members describe what they are attempting with their individual projects. The teacher describes how the members might benefit one another's individual efforts. Subsequent meetings are student directed and are scheduled according to the needs or desires of group members. This type of group should never be forced; rather, the idea is that it is made available as another possible resource for the individual.

SMALL DISCUSSION GROUPS

Small discussion groups that have no connection with individual or group projects can be a desirable asset. These types of groups can have varied kinds of content, sometimes student selected. The primary idea for the existence of small discussion groups is to allow students to remove themselves from their concentrated project work so that they can focus on the subject of creativity itself. To illustrate, the vehicle for discussion might be a book, a movie, or a television situation comedy. Can the group point out principles of creativity that were employed? Life stories of inventors, magicians, composers, artists, and the like seem to appeal to students in a creative behavior class. Favorite comic strips and cartoons serve as excellent vehicles for the analysis of creative behavior. Other possibilities are new toys and games, fashions, household appliances, new machinery of all sorts, new sources of energy—the list is endless.

Discussion groups around such topics are intended to be supportive of the students' own efforts. They should never project a can-you-top-this flavor, for then the purpose would be defeated. Instead, they should inspire and develop the students' self-concept as they acquire a greater and greater under-standing of creative processes and can discover analogies with and strengthen their own.

six

Barriers to Creative Thinking

A. COMMONLY IDENTIFIED BARRIERS

What is it that keeps children, teen-agers, or adults from exercising their creative potential? What is it about ourselves, about the way we think and feel about ourselves, the way we live, the way we relate with other people and to the things that surround us?

Fundamentally, each individual must figure out what barriers to creative expression exist within himself or herself. We all need to discover whether those barriers are internal or external and which are real or imagined. Many barriers are self-imposed. If we assume that we are incapable of some task for some reason or another, we will most likely not attempt it.

Many children in school, for example, who are convinced they will fail, for any of a myriad of reasons, will not try.

And, just as we make negative assumptions about ourselves, we make negative assumptions about others. This becomes a dangerous indictment if one is in a position of influence over others, particularly a teacher. In schools we have a tendency to classify students on a continuum from most capable to least capable. The expectations we have of others are usually the ones they'll live up to. (See *Self-Concept and School Achievement* by W. Purkey.)

The purpose here is to look at some of the sources of the barriers to creative productivity. As each one is discussed, think about whether or not it might apply to you or your children or students. And check yourself on whether or not a particular barrier or category of barriers is a reason you give (or excuse you use!) for your lack of creative expression.

Barriers to utilizing creative potential can be categorized into historical, biological, physiological, sociological, and psychological barriers. Some are discussed at greater length than others because of their bearing on the purpose of this book.

Historical Barriers

In the historical sense, the following examples might give reason for an individual or a society not to attempt the new, to seek another solution, to find a better way. From the ancient Greeks, for example, there was Plato maintaining that history repeats itself. He wrote so convincingly of the circles of civilizations repeating themselves that to many it has seemed futile to attempt any changes. Plato's concept would have us be totally fatalistic and powerless as individuals and as societies.

Analogous is the religious history of mankind and the centuries-old argument of predestination versus free will. So many religions have used fear and conformity as basic tenets. In this country the Puritanical influence has been strong. We are reminded of the early preachers such as Jonathan Edwards and his famous sermon "Sinners in the Hands of an Angry God." Fire and brimstone threats were held over the heads of the general populace so that they would acquiesce to the regulatory teachings of the Church.

On the heels of Puritanism came the Victorian Age, which demonstrated an interpretation of life that allowed little freedom of human behavior and therefore thought. And the influence of Queen Victoria's reign over the British Empire was felt worldwide.

These are but a few examples of historical significance to illustrate external dominance over human thought. It is technological advances, in the recent past and in the present, that leave average people feeling that they have little, if any, control over their own lives.

Biological Barriers

From a biological point of view, some scholars insist that creative ability is a hereditary trait, while others maintain that environment is the major factor. Inherited genes do play a role within the measures of any kinds of intelligence; but too often, in the case of creative intelligence, heredity seems to be more excuse than actual fact.

Physiological Barriers

Physiological barriers can exist through types of brain damage one might incur—through disease, through accident. Or one might have a physical disability of some sort that prevents certain types of productivity. Yet, John Milton was blind and Beethoven was deaf . . .

Sociological Barriers

Most certainly our social environment affects our creative expression. A society is comprised of individuals organized in some manner for the protection and, supposedly, the advancement of its individual members. Problems arise when the organization takes on a life of its own and is responsible for dehumanizing its members, making them feel individually insignificant. A society shares a set of mores and traditions and is characterized by collective activities, interests, and behaviors. Often an individual member feels that it is immoral to deviate from the norm, to appear to differ with the written and unwritten laws of his or her particular group. Whether the society be a nation or a street gang, deviations of behavior from the group's established patterns can evoke punishments or exclusion. Therefore, unique behavior, suggested change, and the like, are considered subversive and threaten the stabiity and security that others derive from group affiliation.

History has demonstrated that when the individual loses a sense of power over his or her own life, a society is ripe for a leader with a dominant personality who advocates group norms and the need to protect those norms. Such appeals to "groupness" and the group's right to sustain itself have been obvious, for example, in Nazi Germany, Communist China, and several African nations.

Also, within a particular sociological setting, whether it be a family, a school, a church, a bridge club, a ball team, there are class systems, designed to keep people in their place, on such bases as age, sex, appearance, ability, background, seniority, right-handedness, and so on.

Social environment is a major factor in our ability to use our creative potential and to express our own uniqueness. Creative expression involves personal risk. Negative reactions to our expressions from our own group can cause us to experience even less self-significance. Often an individual will retreat in order to feel accepted. The implications here are strong for those who attempt to evoke creative behavior through teaching.

Psychological Barriers

Given the foregoing categories of barriers to creative productivity—historical, biological, physiological, and sociological—by far the most signifcant and prevalent barriers are those that are psychological, and these are the ones that demand the most attention from teachers of creative behavior. If we define a barrier as a factor that impedes progress or restricts free movement and give that definition a psychological application, then we are talking about the heart of the teaching profession: What are those elements that impede growth and development and how can they be eliminated or, at least, reduced?

The categories of barriers that have been discussed thus far are, by and large, external factors. They are imposed, for the most part, by forces outside ourselves. Many of them serve well for those who would find reason for not being productive. Some people, in fact, convince themselves that external forces will never allow them to exercise creativity. This in itself is a psychological barrier.

It is difficult to select the best example from literature to illustrate the power of internal forces against one's productivity, so I'd like to suggest a favorite of mine by Emily Dickinson.

WE NEVER KNOW HOW HIGH

We never know how high we are
Till we are called to rise
And then, if we are true to form,
Our statures touch the skies.

The heroism we'd recite
Would be a daily thing,
Did not ourselves the cubits warp
For fear to be a king.[1]

B. EXAMINING YOUR OWN BARRIERS

How do you warp the cubits? Let's turn our attention now to some of the possible internal factors that might hinder your creative output.

First, take this simple math test. Or try it out on your students. Read the directions and allow yourself two minutes to complete the test.

[1] Bianchi, Martha Dickinson and Hampson, Alfred Leete, eds., *Poems by Emily Dickinson* (Boston. Little, Brown & Company, 1957), p. 45

Math Test Directions: Allow yourself two minutes. In the following problems, + means divide, × means subtract, ÷ means add, and − means multiply.

4 + 2 =	2 ÷ 1 =
7 − 3 =	8 + 2 =
8 × 2 =	5 − 4 =
6 + 3 =	4 ÷ 2 =
9 ÷ 3 =	6 − 3 =
8 ÷ 4 =	9 + 3 =
9 × 2 =	6 ÷ 2 =
7 × 2 =	4 − 2 =
8 + 4 =	10 + 5 =
6 × 3 =	12 × 1 =
8 − 2 =	6 ÷ 3 =
12 + 2 =	12 × 2 =
10 ÷ 2 =	3 − 2 =
5 × 3 =	6 + 3 =
4 + 2 =	4 × 2 =
3 × 2 =	8 ÷ 2 =
7 − 2 =	10 + 2 =
7 + 1 =	10 − 2 =
4 × 3 =	10 × 2 =
10 − 5 =	6 + 3 =

Did you finish the test?

Did you read the directions?

If you read and followed the directions and finished the test, you belong to a very small percentage of people.

If you didn't read the directions, it is probably because we are already very test oriented and most directions don't say very much anyway. Also, our society is generally task oriented, and we choose to get on with it. You might also have been pressured by the time limit, so you didn't want to bother with the directions.

This math test serves as an example of habitual, or learned, behavior. Once we have learned the meaning of something—in this case, mathematical symbols—it is difficult to assign new meanings, especially under pressure.

If you attempted to follow the directions, did you work out a system for yourself to facilitate the task, such as taking all the + signs first, the ÷ signs next, and so forth? Or did you attempt to tackle the problems in order, starting at the top of the left-hand column? We have been conditioned, you know, to work from top to bottom and from left to right.

Are you ready for the next one?

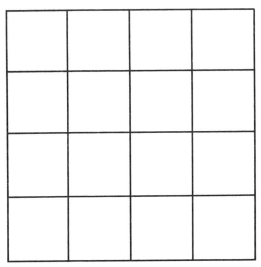

How many squares do you see?

Did you say sixteen? That would be an expected answer. In a traditional classroom, you'd get an *A*. Did you count the outside square and get seventeen? Look at all the squares within the largest square. You'll be able to see thirty squares on this flat plane. (After you discover the 2-by-2 squares, don't neglect the 3-by-3 ones).

So often we give what we assume is the anticipated response, or we fail to look beyond the obvious. Is it wanting to be right? Is it mental laziness or lack of effort? What do you think it is for you?

Take a pencil and a piece of paper. Allow yourself three minutes. Consider your own hand. Write down as many things as you can about your hand.

Did you consider color(s), texture(s), smell(s), taste(s), function(s), mobility, shape(s), design(s), relationships, and so forth? Many times we have more information available to us than we bother to investigate.

If you're not a housing expert, can you name thirty types of dwellings? Try it, you'll surprise yourself.

Did you have some that aren't on this list?

house	birdhouse
duplex	ocean
dormitory	earth
boxcar	nursing home
rooming house	cage
river	prison
monastery	hospital
swamp	aquarium
den	stable
igloo	barn
apartment	coop
hotel	hut
motel	grass shack
condominium	tent
houseboat	palace
trailer	mansion
tree	barracks
cave	pen
nest	corral
doghouse	stall

A majority of times you know much more than you think.

An oldie-but-goodie exercise illustrating an important principle of creative behavior is the Nine Dots Problem.

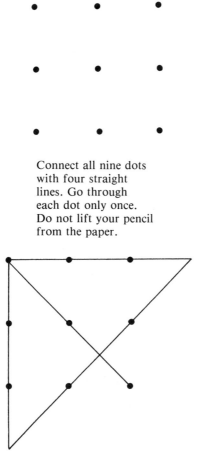

Connect all nine dots
with four straight
lines. Go through
each dot only once.
Do not lift your pencil
from the paper.

The solution to this problem lies in going beyond what appear to be boundaries. Frequently, we assume that boundaries exist when, in fact, they do not. Many people attempt to solve the above problem by staying within the square shape that the dots form. There is nothing in the directions to indicate that one must stay within the shape of the square. The Nine Dots Problem is indicative of boundaries, limitations that are assumed or self-imposed. A crucial phase in developing creative potential is discovering which apparent boundaries or limitations in our lives do not exist in actuality.

Cut a pie into eight
pieces using only
three cuts.

Some possible solutions are these:

Make two cross cuts
and a circular one.

Make two cross cuts
and one horizontally
through the middle.

Make three curving
cuts.

Kinds of things that might have held you back or stymied your students from arriving at these solutions or others like them is that they are unconventional in terms of the way we think about cutting a pie. For one thing, we think of pieces of pie as wedge shaped, and secondly we're usually concerned that the pieces will be the same size.

Perhaps you remember Luchin's Water Jar Experiment. In each of the following problems (numbers 1–8 on the left), you want to end up with a specified number of quarts of water

Problem	Size of Containers	Desired Number of Quarts
1	29, 3	20
2	100, 14, 2	70
3	127, 9, 4	92
4	105, 15, 10	50
5	121, 12, 7	76
6	78, 14, 10	30
7	158, 29, 3	23
8	90, 15, 3	18

(the column on the right). The middle column tells you the size of the containers you have to work with in each problem.

So that in problem 1, you would fill the twenty-nine quart

jar and empty the three-quart jar from it three times, leaving you with twenty quarts. Go ahead and do the rest of the problems.

As I'm sure you have discovered, problems 1 through 6 require that you fill the large container first. Problems 7 and 8 have much simpler solutions. Yet, because a particular strategy has worked well in 1 through 6, one has a tendency to use that same strategy for subsequent problems. That tendency is known as a mind set. Mind sets do not cause much difficulty with harmless exercises such as the one we first went through, but they can be devastatingly restrictive to one's progress toward creative productivity. Think of some mind sets that you are aware of among people you know, institutions you're familiar with, and, by all means, within yourself. How did you react to cutting the pie?

Try this:

$$V || = |$$

Arrange five toothpicks in
the way they appear above.

Obviously, VII does not equal I. By moving just one of the toothpicks can you manage to come up with amounts equal to each other on either side of the = sign?

There are any number of ways this problem can be handled. I'd like to suggest two in order to illustrate a point.

$$V | () = |$$

Remove the circled
toothpick.

$$\sqrt{T} = 1$$

Place the circled toothpick
in a horizontal position as it
appears above—the square
root of one equals one. (Actually, plus or minus one.)

A high school student came up with this one:

$$\sqrt{I} = \triangleright$$

Remove the circled
toothpick, bend it, and
place it on the other side—
six equals six.

Each of these solutions required a transfer in thinking from one category to another. In the first example, from square root to whole number. In the second, from Roman to Arabic numerals. One of the recognized characteristics of a creative person is his or her ability to be flexible. Flexibility as defined in tests for measuring creative ability is the capacity to move with ease from one category to another. Flexibility is a highly regarded trait and is key to increasing one's productivity.

Thus far we have discussed internal factors that inhibit creative behavior such as habit, learned behavior or condition- ing, assumed expectations of others, failure to be aware of all available information, lack of effort or laziness, assumed or self-imposed boundaries or limitations, mind sets, and rigidity or inflexibility. We can add to the list such possibilities as fear of failure or of taking risks, conformity or fear of appearing to be different, fear of ridicule, reliance on authority or following patterns of behavior set by others, routine, comfort, familiar- ity, a need for things to be orderly all the time, superstition, and acceptance of fate, heredity, or one's station in life. Many of these are deliberately overlapping or repetitive to help you identify your own inhibiting factors and those that hold back your students.

seven

Overcoming Barriers
to Creative Thinking

In the preceding chapter, the term *barrier* was defined as a factor that impedes or restricts free movement, and in a psychological context, barriers are those elements that impede growth and development. It is important to temper that statement somewhat at this point so that there are not misconceptions. We need barriers in our lives in some obvious and in some not so obvious ways. Barriers can offer safety checks and quality controls. A totally barrier-free environment could create hazardous chaos. Just as we need guardrails on bridges and turnpikes, psychologically we need the security of certain limitations. In creative thinking, developing convergent skills is just as important as developing divergent skills. The application of convergent skills determines the quality of creative expression in whatever final form that expression might take. The highly skilled creative person uses divergence and convergence equally well. More will be said later with respect to convergence, which is a judgmental skill. The purpose here is to avoid premature judgment at the expense of developing effective divergence.

Becoming skilled in divergence means learning to free our minds for given periods of time to generate thoughts that are not simultaneously censored. For most people that means unlearning some things, dismantling some "protectors" that have been collected throughout our lives.

A number of Allen Funt's *Candid Camera* episodes on TV show Mr. Funt with primary school children. In one of my favorites, he is seen with several young children, one child at a time. He asks the child to "make up a song about happiness." In each case the child does not hesitate. He or she, on the spot, creates both words and music. The new song flows, and the child isn't concerned at the time about the quality of the product, whether the words rhyme or the music stays in one key—the song just happens.

Except in rare cases, an adult given the same task would hedge, laugh nervously, say things like, "I can't sing," "I don't know the first thing about music," "Who me?" or "You've got to be kidding."

Recently I worked with two groups of people on a creative writing exercise. The exercise involves generating lists of possible characters, goals, obstacles, and results as the basic elements of a short story plot and then arbitrarily selecting one idea from each to construct a possible story line. (The process is described more fully later.) One of the groups consisted of college-educated adults, and the other was a dozen or so seven-to-ten-year-olds. When the four elements are selected arbitrarily, sometimes a combination makes immediate logical sense; at other times, a combination at first appears to be so disconnected that a plot couldn't possibly be woven from it. When the second phenomenon occurred for each of these groups, the adults wanted to select new elements; the children immediately responded to the challenge and began supplying links to weave a story together.

Now it's your turn. Try it with your favorite youngsters

too. This activity, called the Morphological Approach to Story Plotting, was developed by Fran Stryker, who, among other things, created the "Lone Ranger."

1. Divide a piece of paper into four columns, as follows:

Character	Goal	Obstacle	Result

2. In the first column, list possible main characters for a short story. Let them be real or imaginary people, animals, inanimate objects, character types—be loose.
3. Disregarding the first column, under "Goal" list things that a character might want to be, to have, or to do.
4. In the third column, list the kinds of things that might get in the way of a character achieving a goal. Obstacles come in many forms: They can be literal brick walls, they can be particular real people, they can be personal traits like shyness. Don't pay attention to what the first two columns contain.
5. In the final column, list ways that things come to an end or ways things turn out. Again, ignore what has already been written in the other columns.
6. Close your eyes and let your pencil fall on one idea from each of the columns.

You now have the four basic elements of a short story plot. Can you write the story? Or would you rather act, draw, sing, mine, or dance it?

If you had just ten items in each column, the possible combinations of elements are ten-thousand. For better or for worse there are ten-thousand potential story plots in front of you. And they are yours. The structure was provided, but the content is yours.

In the group of seven-to-ten-year-olds mentioned previously, an eight-year-old girl began her story like this: "There was a cat named Milk. Milk liked milk. As a matter of fact, Milk liked *Milk* . . ." Milk turned out to be a highly successful and happy cat who went around influencing others to like themselves. A person slightly better known than Milk or his young creator who was aware of the power of a positive self-concept was Leonardo da Vinci. When someone asked him what he considered to be his greatest accomplishment, he replied simply, "Leonardo da Vinci."

Sometimes children and adults too have a hard time pulling together enough of a positive self-concept to feel the sense of personal power it takes to become involved in creative activity. And many times the notion is quite vague as to what it is exactly that holds them back. Perhaps a way to examine that is to look at the many facets of our personalities and our lives and try to pinpoint where the blocks are for each of us. While I was in the midst of studying about Gestalt therapy, I made a connection between some of the tenets of the therapy and Stryker's story-plotting device. My knowledge of Gestalt work is strictly a layperson's, and the application that follows is borrowed from one small segment of a complex psychotherapeutic method.

Gestalt is a German word meaning "the whole." Translated into the common vernacular, when referring to a person, we might say it's "getting it all together." Before one can "get it all together," he or she must recognize, deal with, and attempt to recognize the parts that make up the whole. In personality structures, Gestaltists call these separate parts our subselves. They point out that our subselves can be, at times, in conflict with one another. For example, an aggressive subself and a passive subself might be in conflict. One might prevent the other from acting. Because we have a tendency to want to behave as "whole" persons, it is sometimes confusing to us that our impulses and/or behaviors are quite opposed to what we think we are, should be, or want to be. Gestalt teaches us that it is quite legitimate to be different at different times, and it teaches us to become aware of the parts that make up the whole. (See Fritz Perls, *Gestalt Therapy Verbatim*).

As a first step toward discovering where barriers to creative productivity might lie within your own life, rather than trying to identify the subselves of your personality structure in the Gestalt sense, consider only the various roles in your present life that you choose or are called upon to assume. Start with roles such as teacher, mother, father, husband, wife, son, daughter, Little League coach, Brownie leader, bridge club member, student, neighbor, car pool member, tennis player, artist, choir member, and the like. These are types of roles that are obvious to you and to others who observe you in those roles. Then there are other types of roles you might have assumed that are not so obvious, such as listener, clown, soother, protector, disrupter, dreamer, antagonist, winner, loser, preacher, loner, joiner, catalyst, arbitrator, and so forth. These are among many possible role identities that might be within you.

Altering the basic format slightly, Stryker's model can be used in a personal role-charting way to get at perhaps one's own barriers to creative behavior. Career counselors working with high school students may find this a helpful exercise.

1. This time, divide a piece of paper into five columns, as follows:

Role	Major Goal	Major Obstacle	Usual Result	Desired Result

2. In the first column, list all the possible roles you can think of that are a part of your present life. Be sure to include both the obvious and the not so obvious.

3. As you complete the second column, this time around have the "goal" match the "role" in the first column. You are not looking for arbitrary or chance combinations in this chart; rather, you are attempting to look at the reality of your present situation. Therefore, for each role listed in the first column, write its major goal in the second.

4. From now on in completing the chart, work either horizontally or vertically filling in the last three columns, whichever way seems more comfortable or efficient for you.

As you are going through the activity, write in additional roles that occur to you. When you have finished, you should have a fairly complete picture of the roles in your present life, each role expanded to delineate its major goal, the major obstacle to achieving that goal, the usual results, and what you'd like the results to be.

Hopefully, the completed chart will tell you some things about yourself. In all probability, some of the roles and their subsequent parts on the chart will be perfectly satisfactory to you, the obstacles are readily overcome, and the usual and desired results are the same in content. For others in which dissatisfaction arises, it does well to do some analyzing. There are some general questions you may apply. Is the goal one you have a real investment in? Is the obstacle the literal brick wall type, is it physical or attitudinal, within yourself or external to you? Does the same obstacle appear more than once on your chart?

Remember that the purpose behind this activity is to try to discover clues to what might be barriers to your own creative productivity; in no way is the intent deep-rooted psychoanalysis. It is suggested that you go over your chart with someone who knows you well to see if that person sees you in the same ways you see yourself. One revelation that might occur is that perhaps an obstacle is totally imaginary on your part—one of those assumed limitations. Another possibility is that a particular obstacle, once brought to light, may not be very difficult at all to overcome.

Once you have pinpointed those obstacles seeming to stand in your path to creative productivity, add a sixth column headed "Alternative Behaviors." Think of possible ways you might change your behavior so that "usual" and "desired" results become one and the same. For example, one of your roles depicts you as a member of a group in which your major goal is to make a significant contribution to the group's cause. You've identified the major obstacle to making such a contribution as a basic shyness or feeling of inferiority in comparison with other group members. "Alternative Behaviors" you come up with could be such things as volunteering to chair a committee, determining to speak up more in meetings, introducing a new kind of activity for the group, suggesting that the next meeting be held at your house, and so on. Select an alternative behavior and try it on for size. You may be surprised that a positive action in one area of your life can lead to similar actions elsewhere. And if the initial action leads to a success, you will probably gain the confidence to try other new things. Certainly this is true in the classroom.

Gaining satisfaction in one area of your life often does positively affect other areas. Go back for a moment to the idea of Gestalt, the wholeness of a life experience, the integrating of the separate parts to give one a sense of total well-being. An artist friend of mine has told me about the way in which a painting "happens" for her. The process of getting there, of coming up with a final product, is not a case of knowing what the finished painting will look like. Rather, it is dealing with the separate parts—the brush strokes, the shapes, the tones, the positions—getting each of the parts to a point of success in order for the finished painting to make a whole or integrated statement.

In the personal charting that has been described here, taking off from the Stryker model, we have been dealing with two vital phases of creative processes: analysis and synthesis. Analysis is the breaking down and synthesis is the putting together. It is analogous to any problem-solving process, in which the problem is broken down into workable subproblems. When the subproblems are identified, they can be handled one at a time so that the task is not overwhelming. Once each subproblem is identified and conquered, the synthesis of their solutions or resolutions can begin.

So it is with our own lives. We need to approach the complexities with an analytical eye to become aware of those separate parts that might be causing difficulties in the ability to be creatively expressive. Having raised the difficulty, or barrier, to a level of awareness, one can then work toward a positive resolution of that one barrier. Each single resolution is a step toward synthesizing the whole, toward generating a sense of positive self-concept, of personal power. In addition, the recognition that each life has so many facets allows one the luxury of not demanding total perfection all the time. And it serves as encouragement toward risking oneself. After all, there is a lot of backup depth on the team if one of the players should break a leg.

Often a child feels totally defeated if one segment of his or her life is not going well. Being chosen for a team, getting a part in a play, receiving a gold star on a project can become life-and-death situations. It is important that teachers help youngsters to realize the many facets of their lives in order to help them put so-called failures into perspective. To begin with, the child's feelings about a particular defeat should be neither ignored nor ridiculed. The feelings need to be acknowledged and dealt with before anything resembling perspective can be gained. Acknowledgment of a feeling requires a simple statement, such as "You seem to feel very bad about not being chosen for the team." This type of acknowledgment of a feeling allows the child to talk about it and deal with it. Through talking it out, the intensity of the feeling diminishes, and the teacher can begin the process of helping the child place the event into perspective.

Nothing helps more to overcome feelings of defeat in one area of life than experiencing success in another. When a child suffers a setback of some sort, it is essential that a successful experience becomes available very soon. Assigning a task that you know the child can handle well is a simple solution. It should be the kind of task that will allow the child to be in the spotlight for a short while. The assignment might be to be leader of the recess line, be the one who selects the songs the class will sing during music period, or be the messenger to the main office. If the child has a particular strength, capitalize on that. For example, if he or she is good in art, ask the child to make a special poster for the classroom or to create a decoration for the classroom door.

A child learns to handle a defeat when the effects of the defeat do not last too long. If a setback is allowed to linger for too long a time, it begins to permeate the child's feelings about himself or herself. If it becomes surrounded by successes, the defeat becomes a small part of one's total experience. Subsequently, a child learns to accept occasional defeats as a part of life and is not fearful of risking at some other time. In fact, the child should be encouraged to do so.

eight

Techniques Toward Increasing Ideational Power

Technique, as used in this book, is considered to be an artificial means to an end. A technique is a starting-off point, a tangible diving board to get students accustomed to or to give them a nudge toward releasing a power that is already within them. *The aim is the skill of divergent thinking.* When you completed Stryker's Morphological Approach to Story Plotting, the comment was made that the content of the ten thousand or more possible short story plots was yours, that only the structure for accumulating them was provided. The techniques that follow do the same thing. Their structures and ground rules are intended to set a climate for you and your students to call upon divergent thinking powers. They help to provide an attitudinal framework allowing freedom of thought and negating premature judgment. They provide the means of stretching thinking in the classroom beyond where you thought you could go in ideational efforts. They suggest new directions, associations, adaptations, applications; they increase one's ability to be fluent. Once fluency is increased, other creative traits become apparent in most people. Perhaps it is the confidence one achieves from recognizing the development of this trait.

BRAINSTORMING

Webster's Seventh New Collegiate Dictionary defines a *brainstorm* as "**1:** a violent transient fit of insanity **2 a:** a sudden bright idea **b:** a harebrained idea." A recent pocket addition of *The Merriam-Webster Dictionary* defines *brainstorm* simply as "a sudden burst of inspiration."

Brainstorming as a technique for increasing ideation is a very powerful tool when properly taught and applied. I used to joke that brainstorming was not to be confused with *brainwashing* and *barnstorming;* yet some people's applications might well fall into either or both those two categories. Improperly taught or led, a brainstorming session can become a sham. That thought, along with the idea that in a creative process brainstorming is an end in itself rather than a means to an end, is both damaging and dangerous. Brainstorming as an operational tool is highly valuable in the attitudinal framework its ground rules provide and the ideational abilities it evokes.

Alex F. Osborn, founder of the creative Education Foundation, in his book *Applied Imagination*[1], established four basic ground rules for effective brainstorming sessions. He stated them in the following way:

1. Criticism is ruled out.
2. Freewheeling is welcome.
3. Quantity is wanted.
4. Combination and improvement are sought.

[1] Osborn, Alex F. *Applied Imagination.* Third revised edition. New York. Charles Scribner's Sons, 1963.

Since Osborn's time, there have been refinements but the basic content and implications of these ground rules have not changed.

Most often brainstorming is conducted as a group session, and so the discussion that follows will be geared toward its operation within a group of six to eight people. What I like to call solo brainstorming is an important activity for individual development and will be discussed later.

Although the Osborn rules are stated in a simplistic way, they are not easy to apply. In the first place, each member of the group must sincerely try to abide by them. The power of a brainstorming session occurs when each participant adheres to the rules and assumes the attitudes the rules imply. It is therefore advisable to consider each of the ground rules in some depth.

1. No Criticism   The first tenet of divergent thinking is to rule out any censors for a sustained period of time. Easier said than done; for as a society, we are critically oriented. We have been taught to be critical, and we have been rewarded for our abilities to judge, to be selective, to honor quality. To turn off our critical senses, even for a short period of time, makes us uneasy and quite vulnerable. We suffer all those fears, mentioned earlier, of ridicule, failure, inadequacy, and so forth. It is a tremendous risk of self to be totally uncritical of ourselves and others. But as Osborn so aptly phrased it, we are simply deferring judgment. That is the security blanket, for it helps us understand that removing critical abilities is an expected temporary state. Accepting its temporariness with the knowledge that there will be subsequent judgment before any actions are taken is supportive to our willingness to participate.

Avoiding criticism of others is much easier to employ than avoiding criticism of ourselves. We are our own worst critics, extremely hard on ourselves, often dwelling unfairly on the small bit of some effort that went wrong rather than on the big percentage of that effort that went right. Think about your third-grade spelling tests. What stuck in your mind? The one you got wrong or the nine you got right? Most people have to work very hard in attempting to be noncritical of self.

Criticism of others comes in many different ways, some more subtle than others. Again, the critical orientation of our lives leads us to concentrate more on what others are doing wrong than on what they are doing right. Criticism of others appears in two major varieties: verbal and nonverbal. Verbal criticisms that are less than subtle have been described as "killer phrases." They are the cryptic barbs designed to stop an idea in its tracks. They are definite put-downs and sound something like this: "We tried that last year," "What a crazy idea," "It'll never work here," "You can't be serious," "That's the dumbest thing I ever heard." Condescending killer phrases go like this: "That's cute, but let's try to get some *good* ideas," "Where did you say you went to school?" "We need to try to think of things that will work," "We need to get down to business." Other audible but not necessarily verbal put-downs come in the form of grunts, coughs, snickers, and so on. The nonverbal ones—dirty looks, sidelong glances, a poke in the ribs, thumbs down, a toss of the head, sitting back—are all kinds of gestures whose messages are clear. There is no question about it. It takes a good deal of practice for group members not to demonstrate criticism of one another and for an individual not to censor himself or herself.

2. Freewheeling   The ability to engage in freewheeling thought comes with confidence in the climate set for the task. It's the confidence that you will not be shot down no matter how ridiculous your contribution might seem at the moment of its inception. It's the confidence you gain from hearing others contribute seemingly way-out ideas.

Freewheeling, however, is not encouraged solely to help participants overcome their inhibitions. Freewheeling thoughts move people beyond conventional solutions, often providing the key to solving previously unsolvable problems. The far-out idea can be tempered later or refined into possibly becoming the answer being sought. They offer the new twist, the freshness of approach, the novelty of another way.

3. Quantity   Quantity breeds quality in the sense that there will be more to choose from. If, for example, from the yield of a brainstorming session, 10 percent of the ideas might be workable solutions, it makes sense to generate 100 rather than just 10. Out of that 100, 10 will be yielded that are workable, whereas a total of 10 might yield only one that is workable. Quantity as a goal, in addition to allowing broader selectivity, forces participants to try harder to contribute ideas. Sometimes it is this sheer striving for numbers that offers the best results.

Because quantity is a goal, ideas should be stated briefly; elaboration of them can be effected later. What goes down on paper should be the essence of the thought. In the flurry of the session, it is likely that the same idea might be given more than once. It should be written down each time. To say, "We already have that" is a form of put-down that discourages further contributions.

4. Hitchhiking   One person's idea often sparks a related thought within another person. In fact, one of the greatest benefits of group brainstorming sessions is the way in which participants spur one another on. There is usually excitement and fun and an esprit de corps that develops. It is a healthy, positive experience of working together toward an end. The spirit is cooperative instead of competitive. The climate encourages individuals to be part of the excitement.

At this point, gather a group together and try a brainstorming session. Start with something objective with which everyone is familiar. Someone's belt will serve very well. The object of the session is to think of as many possible uses for the belt as the group can other than its conventional use. Briefly, state the four basic ground rules, set a three-minute time limit, and ask someone merely to tally the number of responses the group gives.

When the session has been completed, have the group process what occurred. Hopefully you came up with a fair number of responses. Immediately the number of responses should be compared with the number of ideas offered in the last group meeting they attended in which brainstorming rules were not in effect. Usually that is a rather dramatic comparison.

Then it is important to examine what exactly went on during the activity according to both individual and group roles. Were there examples of criticism of one another? Did individuals at any time censor their own thinking, feeling perhaps that the response might not be good enough or sound too silly? Could some of the ideas be classified as way out? What examples of hitchhiking were there? Processing helps participants be more effective in subsequent sessions. It sharpens group and individual skills and helps the individuals become aware of how their specific behaviors enhance their own development toward creative productivity.

The role of the leader in a brainstorming session is especially vital, for he or she is reponsible for the group's adhering to the ground rules and yet he or she must serve as facilitator of the process. In the first, gatekeeping responsibility, the leader needs, gently but firmly, to make note of obvious criticisms and must remind participants not to be elaborative about their ideas at this point. As facilitator, the leader has the often difficult task of encouraging without showing approval or disapproval. Perhaps in the leaders' own adherence to the deferred-judgment principle, they can discipline themselves not to be adversely critical, but it is far more difficult not to show approval of a particular contribution. Think about what effect it would have on the group, for example, if the leader says, "Good!" in response to one idea that is put forth. It will inhibit other ideas that might have been forthcoming, participants thinking their next contributions might not measure up. The leader's behavior should portray acknowledgment of each contribution by a nod or by repeating the idea, any kind of appropriate recognition of the contributor without showing either approval or disapproval.

Timing on the part of the leader is crucial. There needs to be allowance for silence, and yet the leader must be tuned into those prolonged moments when silence produces frustration. When that occurs, the leader can facilitate the process by interjecting frames of reference for the participants. For instance, if in working on the belt problem the group seems to have run dry on ideas because they've gotten too many conventional applications out, such as "hold a suitcase together," "hold books together," "dog leash," and so on, then the leader might provide a new frame of reference for their thinking. Providing a setting for the object is one way. Some possibilities follow:

1. You are the props manager for a Broadway production. By mistake all you have to work with are ten thousand belts. How can you use them?
2. Your car broke down, and you are stranded on the desert. All you have is a trunk full of belts. How might you use them?
3. You are stuck with the problem of entertaining a group of children for one hour at a birthday party. All you have is a pile of belts. What can you do?

Another way of providing a frame of reference is to modify or change the object in order to redirect thinking about it.

1. Suppose this belt is ten times its size and strength? What could you use it for?
2. Now it is one-tenth its size. How might it be used?
3. The belt is made out of ice or wood or silver or paper. Now how might you use it?

These frames of reference introduced during brainstorming sessions serve another very important function. They are means of increasing flexibility of thinking. As you recall, flexibility is defined as the ability to change categories.

A brainstorming group that is well practiced probably will not require these kinds of interception. It is advisable, however, for a leader to prepare ahead of time possible frames of reference that could be introduced in the event that the group blocks. Even very experienced groups have occasional lapses. This is especially true when the topic of a brainstorming session is more subjective than objective. Most people don't have a great deal of personal investment in uses for a belt. But questions that involve personal or social subjects, for example, have a decided effect on the way participants attack the brainstorming session. They feel that they must become serious with respect to the nature of the topic, that their ideas must be totally sensible solutions that can be put into effect. Then ability to freewheel is hampered by that judgmental sense they are used to. And yet these are the kinds of topics that most demand fresh approaches, new twists, novel directions.

It rests with the leader to help the group make the transition from something with little or no consequences to something heavier, whose consequences could have important personal or social impact.

Young children are very good at brainstorming. In the first place, they are quite used to adhering to the rules of games and are more able to apply brainstorming rules than are most adults. Many children have already been exposed to the ground rule of "no criticism," for example, through affective education exercises such as Magic Circle. The introduction of a "no criticism" ground rule for brainstorming sessions also has an effect on the general classroom climate. It serves to set a more cooperative tone among the children for other kinds of classroom activities.

Freewheeling and hitchhiking come naturally to children, and most likely do not have to be introduced as brainstorming ground rules for young children. It is best not to clutter the activity with too many rules initially. Subsequent to their having developed the skill of brainstorming, examples of their ability to freewheel and hitchhike in their thinking processes might be pointed out as additional assets.

Quantity should be stressed as a goal to achieve. It's an easy goal to reach with children, and its contribution toward a successful experience is very rewarding for them. Characteristic of youngsters is the tendency to repeat what someone else has just said. It is important to write down what each child says, whether or not it has been said before. For one thing, writing down the repeated idea offers an opportunity to remind the children of the "no criticism" rule for the child who comes up with the killer phrase, "Suzie already said that." Secondly, dignifying each child's response by writing it down, whether or not it is a repeat, is essential to a climate that enhances positive self-concept. Children who see their contributions, original or not, being recorded know that they have been heard. Youngsters will often repeat what has been said because they have seen that the first idea has been accepted and they, too, want their ideas accepted. Having witnessed that their contribution has been acknowledged, children will be less fearful at a later time to risk some original thought.

ATTRIBUTE LISTING

Robert C. Crawford, formerly of the University of Nebraska, is credited with originating the technique of attribute listing.[2] Crawford's device is a good one, for it is similar to breaking down a major problem into subproblems. Instead of attacking a task as a whole, attribute listing suggests that it be broken into its component parts so that each element might be dealt with separately. In a problem-solving situation, being able to articulate a particular subproblem often serves as the key to the major problem solution. Any task is less overwhelming if it can be reduced to workable subpieces.

Crawford's device, however, does more than to suggest a divide-and-conquer approach. It increases ideational possibilities by illustrating the numerous ways in which one might tackle a specific task or problem. Implicit in the use of the term *attribute* is what something already has going for it; it is a positive strategy. Try the following simple exercise:

1. Take a common object such as a ballpoint pen.

2. List as many of its attributes as possible, including size, shape, color, weight, function, and so on.

3. Now, concentrating on one of the attributes you listed, brainstorm possible ways that attribute might be changed or improved upon.

[2] Crawford, Robert P. *The Techniques of Creative Thinking.* New York. Hawthorn Books, Inc., 1954.

If you brainstormed changes or improvements for each of the attributes you were able to list, it is obvious that the number of possible ideas you'd come up with is greatly increased over the number you might generate by working with the ballpoint pen as a whole.

To illustrate the technique of attribute listing, a simple object—a ballpoint pen—was used. It is also a very effective technique when applied to broader questions. For example, if you are or plan to be a teacher, you might use this technique to ideate about the question, "In what ways might the classroom be changed or improved in order to be better conducive to creative behavior?" First, list the attributes the classroom already has. Be sure to go beyond just physical attributes. Attribute listing provides a positive headstart toward solving a problem. Try this suggestion with a classroom with which you are familiar.

Other kinds of applications for attribute listing that can bring positive results are in the human dimension, such as a child who is a behavior problem, problems of relationships among children, teacher-student conflict situations. Before attempting a problem solution, list attributes of the persons(s) or situation and then brainstorm possible solutions for the attribute or attributes that show the greatest promise for alleviating the difficulty.

What present people problem are you aware of right now? Apply the attribute listing technique and see what clues it might bring toward a solution.

Have your students brainstorm the attributes of your classroom just as you might have done with your peers. Ask which attributes might be improved upon. Brainstorm possible improvements. Handling this task with young children might initially be limited to the physical environment, and perhaps one aspect of it, such as the reading corner, for a first time through. One attribute that they may identify is that the reading corner is a quiet spot to sit and read by yourself at a certain time. If that is the attribute they decide to brainstorm for improvements, their suggestions might include cushions to sit on, a rocking chair, plants, a rug, their personal bookmarks for books that must be left there, and so forth.

Some of the conflicts that arise during recess can be readily resolved by youngsters through the use of attribute listing. Consider first the attributes of recess. Then brainstorm improvements of those segments of recess that sometimes cause conflicts or dissatisfactions.

Attribute listing is an especially useful device for improving on individual or group projects in which children are involved. The technique affords an opportunity first to enumerate the attributes of a project and then to brainstorm possible improvements for particular components that need more polish. Types of projects could include science demonstrations, creative writing, a class play, a mural or other visual-arts work, or a home arts project.

FORCED RELATIONSHIPS

Some people subscribe to the idea that there is nothing new under the sun, that anything that appears to be new is merely a new association of what has already existed. New associations or combinations are abundant around us in our everyday world, some very simple and some beyond our ken in complexity. Many things we take for granted were once new associations someone made of existing things. The clock radio or combination storm-and-screen windows are prime examples. Wherever you might be right now, look around and see how many things are associations of two or more things that existed singly before.

When you have done that, mentally place yourself in some other familiar place—your car, the theater, another room in your home or a public building, a park—and think of other things that represent new associations of things that had existed alone before.

Once you have thought of new associations on the object level, think of them on the human level. For instance, within a few short years we have seen desegregation, mainstreaming of the handicapped, and increased sex equity.

The forced-relationship technique, originally developed

by Charles S. Whiting, is a means of helping one to make associations he or she might not have otherwise thought of.[2] Whiting suggests forcing a relationship between two or more normally unrelated objects or ideas as a way of inducing new associations. One simple method for effecting new associations is utilizing a matrix. Items or ideas are listed on the left side and the same items or others are listed across the top. Then, in the box where each one meets another, a new association has been made.

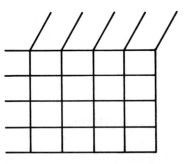

Try one out for yourself using foods and types of preparation. On the left side of a matrix, list some foods you are fond of. Across the top list ways in which different foods are prepared for serving—broiled, chilled, and so on. Then look at where each combination meets in the matrix and see if any new associations suggest something interesting that may not have occurred to you before. You'll no doubt have come up with some associations that don't seem too appealing initially (broiled ice cream?); but, on the other hand, dinner might be very exciting tonight. And to that dinner you could invite some unusual combinations of people that another matrix might suggest to you.

Even people with high creative productivity have found the forced-relationship technique of benefit to them, providing new associations they felt they would not have otherwise made. A former high school student of mine who was already an accomplished poet used a matrix to come up with combinations

[2] Whiting, Charles S. *Creative Thinking* (New York: Reinhold Publishing Corporation, 1958.)

of words to create a particular effect. He wanted to achieve a specific mood by the repeated use of words having an initial sound of *lu*. Using a dictionary, he wrote down on the left side of a matrix all of the nouns he found beginning with the *lu* sound. Across the top he listed all the adjectives he could find. Of all the possible combinations he discovered, he actually used sixty-four of them in a rather lengthy poem he was working on. He was so delighted to have come across another way to approach his already proven talent. That student's exuberance was contagious to others.

An extension of using a matrix in forcing relationships is, of course, Stryker's Morphological Approach to Story Plotting that was mentioned earlier. Morphological analysis is a device that may interest you if the idea of forced relationship appeals to you. If so, look into the work of Myron S. Allen, whose morphological analysis model is one of the best.

Youngsters enjoy using the forced-relationship technique. Have your students look around the classroom to see if they can discover combinations of things that used to exist separately before. Is a student desk and chair one unit? Did someone wear a hooded jacket to school? Have them look out the windows. Are pieces of playground equipment combinations of some sort? Ask them to think about possible combinations that exist in other parts of the school, in a store they are familiar with, or at home.

Have children construct matrices for such things as coming up with new combinations for sandwiches, for making up conversations between characters in different television shows, for inventing new games by combining pieces of equipment from different sports, for inventing a new board or card game combining certain elements of existing games that they enjoy.

CHECKLISTS

The use of checklists as another means for increasing ideation originated with Alex F. Osborn's list of idea-spurring questions. Osborn's questions serve to stretch the thinking when an individual or a group feels ideas have "run dry." The following are Osborn's idea-spurring questions:

1. *Put to other uses?* New ways to use as is? Other uses if modified?
2. *Adapt?* What else is like this? What other ideas does this suggest?
3. *Modify?* Change meaning, color, motion, sound, odor, taste, form, shape? Other changes?
4. *Magnify?* What to add? Greater frequency? Stronger? Larger? Plus ingredient? Multiply?
5. *Minify?* What to subtract? Eliminate? Smaller? Lighter? Slower? Split up? Less frequent?
6. *Substitute?* Who else instead? What else instead? Other place? Other time?
7. *Rearrange?* Other layout? Other sequence? Change pace?
8. *Reverse?* Opposite? Turn it backward? Turn it upside down? Turn it inside out?
9. *Combine?* How about a blend, an assortment? Combine purposes? Combine ideas?[3]

The use of checklists suggests any number of possibilities for increasing students' flexibility in thinking. The Osborn checklist, for instance, offers many opportunities for youngsters to utilize their imaginative powers and suggests numerous activities a teacher might employ. Sample questions you might pose to children based on the Osborn checklist are the following:

1. *Put to other uses?* What could you do with 100 or so roller skate wheels instead of putting them on skates?
2. *Adapt?* How many things can you think of that are like a bathtub?
3. *Modify?* What can you think of that would make going to the dentist more pleasant?

[3] Osborn, Alex F. *Applied Imagination,* 3d Rev. ed. (New York: Charles Scribner's Sons, 1963), pp. 229–90.

4. *Magnify?* What would it be like if your birthday came once a month instead of once a year?
5. *Minify?* What if people were only ten inches tall?
6. *Substitute?* What would happen if bicycles could fly in the air and sail on water?
7. *Rearrange?* What kinds of things would be different if you went to school at night instead of during the day?
8. *Reverse?* What would it be like of everyone walked backward all the time?
9. *Combine?* What kind of invention can you come up with putting together a refrigerator, a radio, and a window?

Once introduced to these kinds of activities, students are quite capable of making up similar ones. Invite them to suggest other activities for the class to try out.

This checklist and others like it help people to exhaust a topic they are working on. They will often provide the new twist, the unique idea that is sought. Checklists also call upon the powers of association that are so facilitating to creative productivity. I have asked my students to create "on-the-spot" checklists that serve to increase their own resourcefulness. When thought processes seem to slow down, leaf through a book, go through your pockets or purse, look out the window, turn the radio on, take a walk, making any associations possible.

Try this exercise in your class:

1. Trace a quarter on a piece of paper filling the page with circles of one-half inch or so.
2. Make a picture out of each figure.
3. After a few minutes, apply a "mental checklist." Mentally place yourself somewhere else, in the gym or the football stadium, at the beach, in the library, in a theater, at the park, on your job, or roam through a department store.

How many additional pictures were you able to evoke? It is possible to force more ideas from your mind.

All of the techniques described here are basic to the fact that you know more than you think you know and that you are more capable of creative thinking than you probably think you are. As mentioned earlier, the term *technique* is thought of as an artificial means to an end, as a way of evoking the divergent abilities already within you. Even after one has become extremely proficient in using his or her creative powers, times arise when techniques need to be called upon, when guidelines need to be reviewed, when reminders about such things as a premature judgment need to be brought to the surface, whether one is working alone or as a member of a group.

It is sometimes scary to realize how much ideational power is within us. As Charlie Brown recently said, "There is no heavier burden than having a great potential." It is also frustrating to recognize capacity and promise within ourselves and then to feel boxed in by what our daily lives seem to hold us to. But overriding these and other possible negative emotions is a new sense of personal freedom and power, a positive attitude that says "Why not?" instead of "Why?" That says, "I'll give it a try," instead of "I could never do that."

We need to convey the attitude of "Why not give it a try?" to children. All of the ideational techniques that have been discussed can be readily modified for youngsters. In fact, these techniques of creative thinking are quite natural to children. It is the adults who need to overcome inhibitions that hinder creative productivity. For children, then, it is a case of teaching them a particular skill that can be deliberately applied, therefore increasing their opportunities to use creative thinking.

nine

From Disorder to Order: A Problem-Solving Process

We've seen pictures of Archimedes running through the streets yelling "Eureka!", we've seen light bulbs appear above the heads of comic strip characters, and we associate these images with the recent pocket dictionary definition mentioned before of *brainstorm*: "a sudden burst of inspiration." We ourselves have experienced the sudden solution to a problem or an answer to a question when our thoughts were on some other subject, perhaps totally unrelated. An answer seems to come from nowhere and when it is least expected, even though there might have been hours or days of concentrated effort directed toward seeking such an answer. This familiar phenomenon is a part of a process operating in the preconscious mind, if you will; that is, the mind has been engaged in a process that has not been apparent on a conscious level.

That occurrence is often referred to as primary creativity, rather like a bolt of lightning instantaneously handing you the answer to a problem whose solution seemed to evade you through sometimes long periods of conscious concentration. Primary creativity, then, is the natural problem-solving process of the mind, with the thinker being unaware consciously that a process is happening. If the mind does naturally function in a problem-solving-process way, would it not be beneficial for people to become consciously aware of what the phases of those processes are in order to call upon them at will? Advocates of what has come to be known as secondary creativity think so. Secondary creativity is raising to a level of conscious awareness those elements—stages of thinking—most common to what has been identified as the natural problem-solving process of the human mind. It is theorized that these stages are preparatory to the mind's having a Eureka! experience. In his book *Grow or Die: The Unifying Principle of Transformation,* George T.L. Land beautifully discusses the processes of growth natural to all living things. He emphasizes that learning for human beings could be much more simplistic if we only became aware of the knowledge and problem-solving ability already within us. Secondary creativity attempts to organize on a conscious level the knowledge we already have and to ask the right questions in order to gain new knowledge. And it attempts to simulate innate problem-solving abilities.

The first discussion of a secondary process here will describe in-depth process stages and suggest activities in each stage that are applicable to adults and older students. While the first discussion deals with suggested content that is relatively objective in nature, the second will be addressed to more difficult subjective material. Finally, ways to help young children use a secondary process are offered.

The secondary creative process suggested here is not the only one. It is a convenient one and is adaptable to many different people and situations. It is not cumbersome and can be expanded or contracted as suits the user's purposes. The five suggested stages are

○ Orientation   ○ Evaluation

○ Preparation   ○ Implementation

○ Ideation

As each stage is defined, experiment with the process by working out some present project or problem in your classroom or at home. Choose something that isn't really major or overly complex and is relatively objective, something comparable to the following:

○ Planning the menu for a dinner party
○ Deciding upon the theme for a classroom Halloween party
○ Rearranging your book collection or reading corner
○ Devising a plan for a schoolyard flower or vegetable garden
○ Designing a costume
○ Landscaping the local park or playground
○ Remodeling or redecorating a room in your home
○ Making the classroom more functional
○ Building sports time into your schedule
○ Doing volunteer work
○ Acquiring an aquarium
○ Planning a special day for a special person
○ Organizing a field trip
○ Learning about birds
○ Improving student physical fitness
○ Playing the piano
○ Planning a playground

Orientation

Orientation in its broadest sense is defining a problem or setting a goal. You could say that any item on the foregoing list is already a problem definition or a goal. However, in order to arrive at results that are truly satisfactory, the class's thinking on the topic needs to be expanded so that one can examine fairly whether or not this is really something the group or an individual want to pursue. Secondly, viewing the question in more depth gives you more to work with, suggesting elements that may serve as keys to an eventual satisfying and workable solution. Put another way, we often do not consider a goal or a problem in enough depth or breadth to give it a fair shake at resolution.

First, take the topic you have selected and write a paragraph or so on how you feel about it. Include such things as

1. What it will mean to have satisfactorily achieved the task—for you, for others
2. Why you want to or have to take on the task
3. How not taking on the task will make you feel
4. What kinds of factors have existed that within yourself and outside yourself have kept you from getting started on it before

In one or two sentences, write the goal you would like to achieve or the problem you would like to solve.

Preparation

Preparation points toward the factual, whereas orientation helps to bring to the surface possible emotional factors involved in beginning to solve a problem or achieve a goal. The orientation stage asks you to deal with sometimes vague feelings that get in the way of tackling something, and it asks you to put on paper the positive emotions that make you want to achieve the task. The preparation stages asks you to lay out in front of you all that is factual about the problem or goal—that which you already know and that which you need to find out. The first part of that—what you already know—is a segment of problem solving in which people do not often give themselves enough credit. Again, it is a case of respecting yourself as a source of knowledge.

The preparation stage, then, is a data-gathering stage. It means providing yourself with enough factual information with respect to the problem or goal so that you have a broad base from which to work.

First, list all the factual information you already have regarding your goal or problem. Include such things as

o Who?

o What?

o When?

o Where?

o How?

Second, list all the factual information you still need to find out. For each item on this list, name possible sources for finding out the information. Don't limit yourself to ordinary sources. Use some of the ideational techniques you've already learned in order to come up with some unusal sources you might tap in addition to conventional ones you've always made use of.

Ideation

Having organized information on both the feeling and the factual levels in the orientation and preparation stages, state the essence of the goal or problem in such a way as to be able to deal with it creatively. That is, in the ideational stage, you are going to apply divergent thinking to arrive at many possible tentative solutions or resolutions. To attempt to create a flow in the way these first three stages operate, let's look at them in the forms of questions.

1. *Orientation* asks "why?" It tries to provide a rationale for pursuing the task and a desire to pursue it by bringing to the surface the emotional factors involved. It hopefully brings out the extenuating circumstances surrounding the potential task and sets a stage of readiness to go on.

2. *Preparation* introduces and organizes the factual realm of the situation. It articulates what you know and what you need to know on a factual informational level. It asks the journalistic questions of who, what, when, where, and how.

3. *Ideation* asks the seeker to explore "In what ways might I . . . ?" The question is open-ended,allowing many possible tentative solutions. Notice that it is not "How can I . . . ?" which might imply that there is only one possible answer. The object in this stage is divergent thinking.

Throughout the three stages, then, different kinds of questions are asked in order to view the situation from different perspectives and to allow expansion of thought toward the final resolution.

In terms of the topic you are presently working on in this exercise, phrase the essence of it in a question that begins with, "In what ways might I . . . ?" and write it down at the top of a blank piece of paper. Conduct a solo brainstorming session and list as quickly as you can all the responses to the question that come to mind. Spend ten minutes as an initial effort. Try hard to apply the brainstorming ground rules:

1. Defer judgment.
2. Freewheel
3. Strive for quantity.
4. Hitchhike on previous ideas.

Don't be concerned if some of your ideas seem conventional. Put them down anyway. They might prove to be very useful; for example, they might be later combined with something else. Really stretch your thinking within the time period.

When the ten minutes have expired, get up and do something else. Then come back and give yourself another ten minutes of ideation in the form of brainstorming. Use your own previous list to hitchhike to or make some new associations from the break experience of having a cup of coffee or walking the dog or whatever you did. Make up your own mental checklist in order to come up with additional ideas. Double, at least, your original list.

If you want to expand possible ideas further in this ideational stage, use any or all of the ideational techniques you've already learned. And if you want to include the thinking of others on this project, gather together a small group of "volunteers" to brainstorm further with you. If you do decide to present the question to a group, don't scare them off with what you've already accomplished alone, and be sure they are schooled in true brainstorming procedures. Also, be willing to answer some questions they may have in regard to your project. It will help them develop a frame of reference toward possible solutions.

Evaluation

Assuming you now have a multitude of ideas that have been generated, the time to become selective has come. Evaluation is convergent thinking. That is, after the ideational efforts have provided you with a whole realm of directions in which you might go, you want to converge on the best one to implement.

Evaluation is a tricky business. It is important not to allow yourself or the class to slip into the yes/no—good/bad syndrome that sometimes tends to kill off some ideas that might have turned out to have had real potential. Before attempting to begin an evaluation process, go back over the pages that contain all the thoughts generated in the ideational stage, and, while the ideas are fresh in your mind, write in any necessary explanatory comments. There may have been abbreviations or symbols that were clear at the time but that may become elusive later on.

If the list of ideas is very extensive, for our purposes here you might want to do an initial screening process to pare them down to a workable number. Never throw any of them away, however, no matter how ridiculous or impossible they may seem for the present situation. They could prove, at some other time and place, to be quite valuable through some sort of modification. Initial screening is really an intuitive activity. Go through your lists and select out those ideas that strike you or the class as being in the realm of possibility for tentative implementation for your situation as you know it. If you think you might have a tendency to be overly conservative in what you select, throw in a few "far-outs" for balance. For the sake of manageability this first time through the process, don't let the list exceed twenty-five ideas in number.

The key to successful evaluation lies in formulating criteria that will judge fairly the potential of each idea. Each criterion is selected according to what or who will be affected if the idea is implemented. To make those kinds of decisions, it is necessary to think through the project you have been working on and make the determinations of who or what will be affected. Generate two lists of possible criteria: one headed "Who" and one headed "What." Don't forget yourself on the "Who" list. As a matter of fact in some cases each criterion could involve yourself. For instance, in a project that deals only with you, you might need criteria such as effects on my time, my budget, my physical self, my attitude, and so forth. You may also find that some criteria should carry more weight than others. Consider weighting them as you make your final selections. Try to settle on just five or six criteria that you will use.

On a large sheet of paper draw a matrix such as was done for the forced-relationships technique. List the ideas that survived your initial screening down the left-hand side, and across the top place your criteria. If you are weighting the criteria, indicate that also by placing "X2" or "X3" in the box with the particular criterion. (See the matrix on page 103 for an example.)

Numerical scoring is the easiest to deal with. You might use the following rating scale:

- o 5 = excellent
- o 4 = very good
- o 3 = good
- o 2 = fair
- o 1 = poor

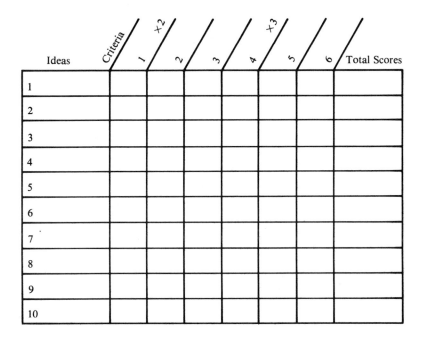

Ideas	Criteria	1	×2 2	3	4	×3 5	6	Total Scores
1								
2								
3								
4								
5								
6								
7								
8								
9								
10								

It seems to average out in the long run to assign a "3" in a case where your response would be "not applicable." When doing the ratings, move in a vertical rather than a horizontal direction. That allows you to keep one criterion as a frame of reference for judging each idea against it. Moving horizontally might lead you to favor one idea or to be negative about it all the way across. The vertical approach also makes it easier to deal with weighted criteria. Begin, then, with criterion 1 and give each idea down the left-hand side a numerical rating according to the rating scale suggested above. When all ideas have been given a number value against that criterion, go on to criterion 2, and so forth.

When all ideas have been judged against all criteria, add together the scores across for each idea and place the total in the column provided at the far right. Then circle the top three or five total scores to see which of your ideas faired best according to this method of evaluation. You may be surprised by the ones that come out on top. They may not be the ones that you anticipated would rank the highest. Yet the completed matrix represents your best judgment in selecting and weighting criteria in order to project the effects of implementation of any of the ideas. This whole evaluation process does allow you to be far more objective about your ideas than you might have been otherwise.

Implementation

All of the above has been to no avail if you don't take any action. Hopefully you have worked through this process on a project you have really wanted or needed to actualize. If that has been true, then an implementation plan is your next step. And because you have carefully processed your problem or goal from start to finish, the probability of success is very high. It is a temptation for some, for instance, to get excited about some of the ideas generated in the third, or ideational, stage and want to implement them immediately. The well-processed evaluation stage, however, affords a much greater probability of success in implementation.

It should be stated at this point that these five stages are not static. The wise problem solver will become aware of the fact that working on the third stage, for example, might suggest vital information for the first and second stages. So he or she goes back and fills in the missing parts. The more complete each stage is, the greater the opportunity for arriving at a highly satisfactory resolution. Particularly in projects of broader scope or greater complexity is it important to keep the cyclical nature of the process in mind.

A plan of implementation should be drawn up. It need not be extremely elaborate, but it does need to be organized so that it can be carried out. Depending on the nature of your project, select from the following questions those that apply in order to plan your implementation:

1. What has to happen before anything else can?
2. Who else will be involved?
3. Do I need to convince anyone else of my ideas?

4. What strategy for convincing shall I use?
5. What materials do I need to assemble?
6. What rearranging of schedules are necessary?
7. Does anything else have to be sacrificed in order to implement this idea?
8. When is the best time to start?
9. Is the place for it to happen of concern?
10. What is the best order for the phases of the implementation?

Add other questions that are pertinent to your situation.

Good luck, and enjoy the fruits of your labors.

THE PROCESS APPLIED
TO MORE SUBJECTIVE MATERIAL

When concerns are more objective in nature, it is easier to apply a process in secondary creativity than it is when the concerns are more subjective, closer to you personally. Your own emotions play a much larger part. When you are directly involved and the concern is a personally serious one, it is difficult not to employ, for example, all that is judgmental within you during the ideational stage, and it is not uncommon to have difficulty stating the precise problem or goal clearly. It is also quite natural for you to be more pessimistic about arriving at a satisfying and successful resolution.

With the knowledge that these negative forces may operate against you, and with your concentration set on resisting them, the following suggestions are made within the five-stage process to help you to be as successful with subjective material as you have been with objective material. In reality, application of this process to subjective concerns can provide you with a tangible, organized method toward achieving a goal or solving a problem. The organization itself helps you to approach the topic objectively, while within its procedures sensitivity to your feelings is acknowledged.

Orientation

Subjective material will naturally be more difficult to pin down into a problem definition, more difficult to be articulate about, more vague in concept. Your approach, therefore, needs to aid you in making a precise statement about what it is you would like to achieve. Writing or talking about your concerns is often cathartic. If getting it down on paper is a major hurdle for you, use a tape recorder in this step and talk it out.

1. In thirty to forty-five minutes in a stream-of-consciousness manner, write down everything you know that is related to the goal you would like to achieve. Include feelings you have about it, feelings you think others have, factual information, things you suspect might be true, causes and effects, and so on. Don't concern yourself with such things as sentence structure, organization, or spelling. The important thing is to get the thoughts or feelings down. If you seem to run out of things to write down, go back over what you have already written and elaborate on one or more points you have already mentioned.

2. Leave your writing for a while and do something completely different, preferably something physical that doesn't require much thought on your part.

3. Come back and spend at least another fifteen minutes adding to what you have written.

4. Go back over what you have written, and with a different color pen, mark with an *A* those elements that seem to you to be of major importance. Mark with a *B* elements of lesser importance. And mark with a *C* those things you feel might be eliminated, at least for now.

5. On another piece of paper, list the *A*'s in one column and the *B*'s in another.

6. Prioritize the lists in each column by ranking them according to their apparent importance, that is, rank number 1 the most important, and so forth.

7. Make an outline of major elements and their subdivisions as you see them.

8. Using the outline, write a news story in the third person (your name, he or she) as if you were writing about some-one else. A news story is supposed to contain only facts, which follow an organization of most to least important. Try to avoid any opinion or the use of loaded adjectives and adverbs.

9. Are there facts missing in the news story that are essential to achieving a goal or solving a problem eventually? Make a list of questions beginning with "Who," "What," "When," "Where" that it would be helpful to know. Next to each quesiton, name all the possible sources you can think of for obtaining answers.

10. Convert each factual-type question into a creative-type one, that is, "In what ways might I . . .?"

11. Select one of the creative-type questions that you would like to work on first.

The orientation stage this time, when dealing with sub-jective material, has included some procedures identified as parts of the preparation and ideational stages while working on more objective topics. These are deliberate inclusions in the first stage, because in tackling personally oriented topics, people might become discouraged with, say, working on just trying to define the problem. Often in these kinds of subjective topics, the individual will feel that the problem is clearly de-fined and that it seems too overwhelming for him or her to be able to do anything about. The procedures in the orientation stage, though cumbersome, are designed to have individuals re-move themselves as far as possible away from the problem and, by the end of this stage, to have next steps clearly apparent.

Preparation

This time the preparation stage involves gathering the in-formation you want and have already identified as being need-ed. The use of a creative-type question is intended for you to ex-tend your thinking with respect to possible sources of informa-tion. This is an area in which we often limit ourselves unnecessarily. A former student of mine determined his career choice through using the yellow pages of a telephone book!

Take whatever amount of time is required to find answers to the factual questions you have raised. The factual information you gather will put you well on your way to a final resolution. The more information you have, the more you'll have to work with; for you will be opening new doors to knowledge of and awareness about the topic. You are building a foundation from which to work toward solid conclusions. Questions you will seek answers to in the ideational stage will be well grounded in the work you have done in the preparation stage and therefore will show greater promise for solution. If your efforts are superficial, so will be the results. If your efforts have depth, the results will too.

Ideation

Prepare major questions or subdivisions of them for brainstorming. Remember, if you are going to conduct a group brainstorming session, always conduct a solo session yourself ahead of time. This does two things: (1) it continues to remind you to respect and make use of yourself as a source so that you don't depend totally on outside sources; and (2) it helps you better explain what it is you'd like to have the group do.

When preparing to conduct a group session, write a paragraph that begins with the creative-type question followed by factual information that will help the group focus on exactly what you are asking. Answer any other preliminary questions the group might have.

Use other ideational techniques as they apply. Ideate major and minor segments of your topic as you deem necessary and/or desirable. Some questions you have posed may answer themselves through your efforts on other questions.

Evaluation

Initial screenings and matrix evaluations should be applied accordingly. Criteria selection should receive careful attention, especially in the area of subjective material. Brainstorming for possible criteria is a good idea so that all bases are covered. It is crucial that at this stage you give all generated ideas a fair shake and not fall back into premature judging because of the personal nature of your topic.

Implementation

Devise a solid plan for implementation from all of your efforts. Ask the right questions ahead of time to ensure success. And, by all means, put the plan into action.

USING THE PROCESS WITH YOUNG CHILDREN

When introducing a problem-solving process to young children, it is advisable to work with content that all of the children can readily relate with, that is, a common school problem that they share or a goal the class would like to achieve. Some examples might be the following:

- How to handle lost and found articles
- How to distribute classroom chores fairly
- How to arrange for watering the plants and caring for classroom pets during vacations
- How to see that everyone has a turn with playground equipment during recess
- How to give everyone a chance to use the headsets in the listening center or the laboratory equipment in the science center
- How to improve upon the way the children enter the classroom in the morning
- How to prepare for parents' night
- How to have a toy drive for less fortunate children
- How to plan an assembly program

Orientation

First, have the class list projects they might like to work on as a group and/or problems dealing with the classroom that they feel need to be solved. Provide a few examples to get them started. Depending upon the teacher's particular situation, it might be more appropos to preselect a topic for the children to work on the first time through. The illustration given here of using the process with young children uses the topic "How to Improve upon the Way Children Enter the Classroom in the Morning."

The teacher might begin by expressing his or her own concerns about the topic and ask the children to express any of their concerns about it. Be certain to avert anything resembling finger pointing and help the students to gain an objectivity about putting the major concern in a framework of problem solving and not one of placing blame. Elaboration of the concerns suggests the subproblems. List them and talk about their being the separate parts of the larger problem. Subproblems might be shouting, pushing, everyone trying to get through the door at once, books being dropped, crowding one another while trying to take boots off, bus riders and walkers arriving at different times, big sisters and brothers delivering forgotten lunches, the bell ringing before a game is finished, and so on.

The orientation phase of problem solving does bring to the surface possible emotional factors involved in the major concern. Perhaps feelings of disturbance and unhappiness have prevailed. Breaking it down into subparts helps the children to realize what the smaller things are that contribute to the general unpleasantness. It also helps them see that with the subproblems handled separately, the overall problem seems more solvable. Secondly, recognizing the existence of several of the subproblems contributes to the factual information they will need in the preparation stage.

Preparation

This stage deals with known facts as well as factual-information gaps. It is a good idea for you and the class to review together differences between facts and opinions, facts and guesses, facts and rumors. Then ask them to look at the sub-problems they've named and decide which ones are facts. They can all be listed as facts. Can they think of any other facts? At this point, guide them toward looking at facts that surround the actual occurrences that were listed as subproblems. Help them to expand their information base by enumerating such things as

- The time the bell for entering the classroom rings
- The time buses arrive
- The time walkers arrive
- The kinds of things children do outside the building before the bell rings
- Special school rules for inclement weather, and the like

The next step is to ask the children if there are other facts they think it would be helpful to know. For each factual question they offer, ask them to figure out where or from whom they can find answers. Different children can volunteer or be assigned to bring the answers to the next session.

Ideation

Have the students state creative-type questions ("In what ways might we . . .?") from subproblems they have identified or factual information they have gathered. Select specific questions to be worked on by small groups or the whole class.

Apply brainstorming, attribute listing, or any of the other ideational techniques that seem appropriate.

Evaluation

In their small groups or with the whole class, have the children determine criteria by which to judge their ideas. It would be a good idea to spend some time helping the children to ascertain the difference between "voting" for an idea because they like it and judging the potential of an idea by measuring it against selected criteria. As you bring up each possible criterion, use the phrase *effect on;* this helps children to understand what criteria are. Although weighting criteria, as was discussed before, may be too difficult a concept for some young children, having them work with an evaluation matrix is not. For a first time around, limit criteria to three or four and ideas to be judged to ten to twenty, depending upon the children's ages and abilities.

Implementation

The children will enjoy devising a plan of action for the idea(s) that were judged the best. Determining what must be done first, how the responsibilities are to be shared, and so on, will lead them into a successful experience.

This entire process has worked well for teachers of young children. As is obvious, there are numerous types of learning experiences to be gained in addition to expanding children's creative thinking abilitites.

ten

Developing Sensitivity

Knowledge of a problem-solving process is of little value if one is insensitive to problems that need to be solved. A process that is a method for achieving a goal is useless to the person who has no goals. Yet we are surrounded by problems that need to be solved, problems that range on a continuum from global, or universal, concerns to personal ones. We have universal problems in connection with the Space Age, in which we live; we have worldwide problems of famine, diseases, energy, natural resources, pollution, cold wars, not-so-cold wars, overpopulation, currency and gold standards, prejudice, greed, crime, natural disasters; we have national, state, and local problems; we have family problems, problems among our friends, and individual personal problems. For as many problems that exist there are just as many goals that can be set.

Developing sensitivity is not something that is necessary for all people. In fact, some people are overly sensitive, to a point where knowledge of existing problems is overwhelming and almost paralyzing. These individuals are ones who need to be helped to become more active than passive, less fatalistic and more goal oriented. The next level of sensitive people exact a balance between what they sense needs to be done and what they can do toward getting it done. And finally, in this gross oversimplification, there are those who remain insensitive, either by learned behavior or because of a lack of opportunity to become sensitive. For some, sensitivity or lack of it has deep-seated psychological underpinnings. For others, insensitivity through learned behavior has been a necessity for reasons of survival. No judgments are being made here.

The discussion that follows is directed toward those people, especially teachers and parents, who want to heighten their sensitivity to their surroundings, who want to become aware of opportunities to solve problems and set meaningful goals, who want to counteract within themselves feelings of uselessness, boredom, inadequacy, lethargy, and so on. Or perhaps you want to help your children develop more constructive feelings.

Becoming aware of a need—whether it be a human need, one's own or someone else's, an area of society's or all of society's, or whether it be a personal social problem, a practical problem, or a need for aesthetic expression—is what Dr. Sidney J. Parnes of the Creative Education Foundation refers to as developing "a constructive discontent." Usually recognition of needs leads one to attempt to fulfill them. I say "usually" for I am reminded of a seventh-grade boy who used to enjoy saying, "I'd like to do something about the apathy around here, but I don't feel like it." Whatever your purposes, perhaps some of the following will open some doors to both awareness and opportunity.

Try the first three exercises on your own. The remaining seven exercises are written first on an adult level or for older students; a second version of each of these is suggested for youngsters.

AWARENESS

1. Yesterday's Paper Dig out yesterday's daily news-paper, and on a separate piece of blank paper write down each headline that indicates some sort of problem.

Then categorize the headlines in the following way according to their scope:

A. Outerspace or universal
B. Global or international
C. National
D. Statewide
E. Local

Then give each headline a second rating according to its effect on people. The number of people affected are

1. A million or more
2. A thousand or more
3. A hundred or more
4. Ten or more
5. Less than ten

Rate the severity of the consequences of the problem if not yet solved:

a. Extremely severe
b. Very severe
c. Severe
d. Somewhat severe
e. Not very severe

2. Today's Paper Take today's newspaper, if you haven't read it yet, or a magazine you have not yet read and locate all the pictures, covering over any surrounding headlines or captions before you have had a chance to read these.

On a separate piece of paper, write what you think the headline or caption will say.

3. Tonight's Television Newscast   As you watch tonight's television newscasts, write down everything the newscasters report that is *not* a problem. Don't forget the weather forecast.

4. Public Place   The next time you are in a public place —a bank, a post office, a park, a bus station, a theater—observe (but don't eavesdrop on) people. Try to figure out from facial expressions, gestures, and postures what they are thinking and feeling.

When you are in a public place with your children, stand a distance away from other people and ask the children to guess thoughts and feelings people might reveal through their facial expressions and gestures. Ask the children if they can tell if the people are happy, sad, angry. Ask them why they think so. In the classroom the use of creative dramatics is very effective in developing children's sensitivity to the thoughts and feelings of others. Have two or three children pantomine a situation and have the others guess thoughts and feelings. The situations can be quite simple—two people talking in a car, a mother comforting a child with a scraped knee, three children building a sand castle on the beach, and so forth. Have the children build a complete story around the situation, that is, as a result of what they observe going on now, suggest what might have happened before and what might happen afterward.

5. Music   Listen to some music you've never heard before, preferably several very different kinds of pieces. Ask yourself what frame of mind each composer might have been in at the time the piece was written. Try to guess what events in his or her life might have caused that frame of mind.

In addition to discussing with the children the composer's possible frame of mind, have them act out or draw a picture depicting the mood the music suggests to them.

6. *Art* Look at a number of abstract paintings in a gallery or in a book. What mood does each artist attempt to convey? What elements of the painting tell you something about the mood?

With children this exercise need not be limited to abstract painting. Realistic and impressionistic pieces also work very well. If the paintings you select to use with children have people in them, make certain to go beyond postures and facial expressions as indicators of the mood the artist is attempting to convey. Consider such things as color, shading, choice of objects included, and the size of the people in the painting compared with other things.

7. *Scenes* Mentally picture a peaceful country scene or a quiet city street early in the morning. Predict what problems might erupt within a few hours or what problems might already exist that you are initially unaware of.

The key to using this exercise with young children is to provide a scene for them that is very familiar. Much that is involved in developing sensitivity is sharpening one's ability to predict possible problems, to sense what might occur so that one is not always in a position of being the passive reactor to problems that arise. School scenes that can be used are the cafeteria before lunch, the auditorium before an assembly program, the playground before recess, and the parking lot before buses and cars arrive at the end of the day. Allow the children to elaborate on all of the details of what they know will occur through past experience. Then ask, "What else could happen?" In this way their imaginations are stretched and their skills in predicting are increased.

8. *Short Story* Read a portion of a short story with which you are unfamiliar. After a character has been introduced or a scene has been set, try to anticipate what problems will be encountered in the following paragraphs.

As you try this exercise with a story appropriate to the children's age levels, ask them what clues they've gotten from the portion of the story that has been read that supports their predictions. This will help them to develop the skill of seeking out clues. Children's mystery stories provide ideal material for this exercise. A second level of sensitivity can be included after the children feel comfortable with this exercise. Divide the youngsters into small groups and ask each group to arrive at a consensus with respect to the way the story will end. It is an opportunity to help them develop sensitivity toward one another.

9. *Ordinary Situations*   After each of the situations described below, try to recognize potential needs from events that might occur.

1. A boy with his dog sitting on a river bank fishing on a bright summer day
2. A bank teller getting off the subway, as she has done for the past twenty years
3. A clergyman about to begin a worship service
4. A teacher reading the morning announcements
5. Two teen-agers sitting in a car waiting for a red light to change

In addition to some of the situations described above, which youngsters are capable of handling, are the following:

1. A girl waiting for the school bus in front of her house
2. A boy standing outside the fence waiting for the town swimming pool to open
3. A father walking out of the house in the morning to get in his car and drive to work
4. A baby-sitter saying good-bye at the door to the children's parents
5. A crossing guard walking to his or her corner in the morning

10. *Someone Else's Shoes*   We often use the phrase, "If I were in your shoes . . ." Wear some of these shoes for a while.

1. Eat lunch today blindfolded.

2. Watch a television drama without turning up the volume.

3. Arrange to spend one-half day in a wheelchair.

4. Communicate for one-half day without using speech

5. Switch places with your friend or spouse for a day.

6. Switch places with a child for a day.

Kinds of activities for children that can help them understand someone else's situation need to be carefully selected. Activities like the first four listed above, which deal with being handicapped, might be modified for children, especially if some handicapped children are to be mainstreamed into your classroom. Caution should be exercised, however, so that the children aren't frightened. A few minutes wearing a blindfold or watching television with the sound turned off, for example, can be quite effective in building empathy for handicapped children if handled in accordance with the maturity of the children you work with. Other activities that can help children try on someone else's shoes are the following:

1. Pretend that you are a new student in this school.

2. Ask the school bus driver or the crossing guard what it feels like to be responsible for the safety of so many children.

3. Talk to a cafeteria worker or a janitor about what their jobs are like.

4. If you are an only child, talk with someone from a large family about what his or her family life is like, and vice versa.

5. If you live in an apartment, compare notes with someone who lives in a house.

6. If you ride a school bus, talk with someone who walks to school.

FOCUS

There are times when problems seem too vague or complex or limited in scope or too out of our reach to do anything about them, even though we might have direct involvement. It is easy to become discouraged.

Vagueness is that feeling that there is something wrong, but you can't quite put your finger on what it is. You sense a fuzziness, an uneasiness, but a target is elusive. In the preceding chapter, which dealt with the application of a secondary creative process to subjective material, a means for beginning to verbalize subject matter that is very personally close was suggested. The same type of approach is possible with vague feelings that arise whether or not you are personally related to the situation. Once again, then, it is suggested that you designate a time period, preferably more than half an hour, and write down or speak into a tape recorder the sensations you are experiencing with respect to the situation. In addition to your feelings about it, include anything you know or think you know about the situation.

When the time period you've allowed yourself is up, leave the task and do something else. Then come back and spend another fifteen minutes, at least, making additions or expanding on some phase(s) you have already included. The stretching for expression is important. Even if what you add is a reiteration of things already expressed, saying it again in different words might offer some useful clues.

Then, using either facts or feelings from the context of what you have written or recorded, write as many divergent questions as you can that begin with, "In what ways might I . . . ?" Possible endings for this sentence stub are

- find out who can be of help?
- use my own resources and skills to tackle the situation?
- discover what other resources are available?
- divide this situation into workable subproblems?
- check out the validity of what I think are facts?

o substitute a more precise word for each rather vague feeling word I've used?

Make a list of your own endings. Then brainstorm possibilities for each of the questions. You should now have enough material to work with so that what had been vague or fuzzy is beginning to come into focus.

Children often become quite frustrated when they are unable to focus on what seems to be wrong. They can be helped if you encourage them to verbalize the situation. As they talk, listen for what is fact and what is feeling. Repeating some of the key statements to help separate fact from feeling also lets children know they have been heard, which is very important as they attempt to focus. Such reiteration as "Bonnie came right up to you and took the ball" and "You were feeling very angry" help children to organize their thoughts and feelings. Then ask if there is anything else they can think of. "In what ways might I . . . ?" questions can then be generated, with one or more of them to be brainstormed. This process of moving from confused frustration to one of focused articulation gives children a sense of personal power over situations in their own lives.

A problem that seems to be too complex needs to be broken down into subdivisions that can be attacked individually. In an earlier exercise, you were asked to list and categorize in three different ways the problems suggested by the headlines in a daily newspaper. Select one headline that implies a rather broad scope, and using only the headline information, list as many as you can of the subproblems that you think this major problem might contain. Take some of the other headlines, regardless of their scope, and do the same thing.

Now take the subproblems you've identified from one of the headlines and suggest a sequential order in which they might be placed so that you can approach problem solving systematically. In other words, determine which subproblems would have to be solved before others could be attempted.

Problems that are too limited by their definition preclude limited solutions. Sometimes we trap ourselves into very few alternatives by virtue of the words—particularly the verbs—that we use. Suppose, for example, you have been putting off writing a letter that is difficult to write for one reason or another. Instead of saying "How to write a specific letter?" you could use "How to communicate?" or "How to get across certain thoughts, feelings, or information?" "Writing a letter" limits the way to achieve the goal, while "communicating thoughts, feelings, information" opens up a whole range of approaches you might employ. Instead of "How to get along with my brother?" try "How to achieve peaceful relationships with others?" Instead of "How to catch mice?" try "How to get rid of them?"

Taking key words, especially the verbs, in a problem statement and expanding their meanings allows many more opportunities for novel and, perhaps, workable solutions. A thesaurus or dictionary is a useful tool for this activity. Try expanding the following:

- How to get to work on time?
- How to sew a patch on a shirt?
- How to glue together a broken toy?
- How to teach children respect for others?

Writing each statement several times to allow a broader scope of possible approaches to the problem will suggest to you the many different kinds of ways that you might arrive at solutions. If the statement is very narrow, your opportunities will be very limited.

Another approach is asking "Why?" after each problem statement you write and writing another question that implies an answer. For example,

- How to lose weight?
  Why?
- How to be thinner?
  Why?
- How to be more attractive?
  Why?

○ How to feel more comfortable speaking before a group?
   Why?
○ How to feel good about myself?

A sequence for children might be:

○ How to do better in math?
   Why?
○ How to have a better report card?
   Why
○ How to make my parents happier?
   Why?
○ How to make myself happier?

This kind of exercise attempts to help you and your students focus on what is underlying the problem statements you've written. It can suggest the true motivation for wanting to achieve the goal. It can help get at the real problem that exists by taking it out of the limiting, and sometimes seemingly hopeless, context in which it has existed.

We often futilely seek solutions to ill-defined problems because we have not dug deep enough to discover what the real problem is. For instance, if we see a group of youngsters in a ballgame on a playground and one child is standing on the side just watching, we might make assumptions that aren't true, such as

○ There's a new kid on the block and the others haven't invited her or him to play.
○ The child is short or black or fat or the opposite sex, and the other kids won't let him or her play.
○ The child who is on the sidelines is a sissy.

We jump to premature conclusions about the situation without knowing enough about it. What are some other reasons that the child might be standing alone on the sidelines? What are some ways you could find out? Can you remember any events in your own life in which you drew erroneous conclusions prematurely? Have there been times when you have suffered because some-one else made assumptions that weren't true?

Precise problem definitions are elusive, yet essential. Sensitivity on the part of the potential problem solver that his or her first definition might not be on target is vital to the eventual solution. The kinds of activities that have been suggested here are designed to sharpen skills of divergence and convergence as they apply to becoming more sensitive to both the existence of problems and their accurately stated definitions. Decision making is a way of life. We make dozens of decisions every day. Some are automatic and need to be. Others, however, deserve more time, thought, sensitivity, and refined definition. And it behooves us to develop these attributes in youngsters.

eleven

Measuring
Student Growth

In classes designed to evoke creative behavior, it is important for the student to be able to see his or her own growth in processes as well as in end products. A good deal of emphasis has been placed on self-awareness, on conscious knowledge of mental and emotional processes within oneself. Students need to have available tangible evidence of their progress. They have learned to recognize evaluation as an important and necessary part of the creative process. They need to know whether or not efforts expended have been worthwhile. Indeed, it is important also for the teacher to know whether or not his or her efforts on behalf of the students have been worthwhile. Because following one's own growth and development has been emphasized, each measure of growth and development mentioned is one in which the student actively participates. Many benefits can be derived from this approach to assessment. Not least among them is a sense of responsibility for one's own learning.

PRETESTING AND POSTTESTING

Prior to introducing any work toward evoking creative behavior, a creative ability test can be administered. A similar test can be administered when the class has been completed. What you choose to use as a creative ability test depends upon the degree of formality attached to your purposes. If you are engaged in research, then one or more of the validated tests available should be used. In fact, since creativity is a very complex behavior affected by many factors, the use of only one of the available creative thinking tests will probably be too limiting for formal research purposes. Gary A. Davis, in *It's Your Imagination*, lists numerous available creativity tests. If the area of testing for creative thinking abilities is new to you, this publication might serve as a good introduction. Certainly creative thinking tests that have been developed by Torrance, Guilford, and Wallach-Kagan should be investigated.

If your purposes are less formal, then constructing your own tests as you do in other subject areas is legitimate. The tests, naturally, should address themselves to the kinds of activities you plan to introduce to your students. With your guidance initially, students can score their own tests and usually are eager to do so. The creative abilities that are fairly easy to score with your students are fluency, flexibility, originality, and elaboration. It is preferable to include some nonverbal items along with the verbal ones to account for students whose learning styles are oriented to the nonverbal. A sample test with possible categories of creative thinking you might use follows.

1. Alternative Solutions to Problems
   a. Describe a problem situation such as a major traffic snarl during rush hour at a particular intersection with which the students are familiar.

   b. Have them write down as many possible solutions to the problems as they can.
   c. Allow six minutes.
2. Results of Given Solutions
   a. Describe a situation that may have any number of ramifications. For example, a mischievous student has set off a fire alarm in a large junior high school during a period of the school day that is lunch hour for some and classes for others.
   b. Have students write down as many possible results as they can think of.
   c. Allow four minutes.
3. Giving Reasons or Explanations
   a. Propose a statement that students are to assume is true. For instance, students who walk to school instead of riding in a bus or a car achieve higher grades.
   b. Have them give as many reasons or explanations as to why this statement might be true.
   c. Allow three minutes
4. Possible Uses for Common Objects
   a. Name some common object, such as a wooden ruler, throwaway soda bottles, or coffee cups with the handles missing.
   b. Have them think of as many possible uses for the object(s) as they can.
   c. Allow three minutes.

5. Shapes
   a. Provide a page that repeats the same shape (circles, squares, or triangles) of the same size.
   b. Ask students to make as many interesting and different pictures as they can using the shapes. Have them label each picture.
   c. Allow six minutes.
6. Incomplete Figures
   a. Draw some lines (straight or curved) that have no closure.

    b. Have students make an interesting picture from each incomplete figure.

    c. Allow six minutes.

Scoring procedures for the above nonscientific approach will yield four scores on each of the above six categories. Use the ones that seem appropriate for your students. Scores can be yielded in the following areas and ways:

1. *Fluency:* The actual number of ideas or solutions.

2. *Flexibility:* The actual number of different kinds or categories of ideas. For example, different categories of usage for coffee cups without handles could be (a) as a container; (b) as a decoration; (c) as broken pieces for the making of mosaics; (d) glued together to make a table; and so on.

3. *Originality:* The degree to which ideas are unique as compared with the ideas of others in the group. If you have twenty students in your class and only one came up with a particular idea, that student's score would be twenty. If half the class had the same idea, the score would be ten; and if everyone had the same idea, the score would be zero. If, for instance, everyone drew a baseball on a circles test question, that item on the page would be zero for an originality score.

4. *Elaboration:* The number of details provided in any one response. For example, for the question involving a fire alarm going off, the detailed response might be (a) students in a third-floor classroom; (b) came down a fire escape; (c) waving their tests papers; (d) shouting, "Too bad!"

A test results sheet might look like this:

Results of Creative Ability Tests

	I Pre|Post	II Pre|Post	III Pre|Post	IV Pre|Post	V Pre|Post	VI Pre|Post	TOTALS Pre|Post
Fluency							
Flexibility							
Originality							
Elaboration							

Pretesting and posttesting for creative thinking ability can be as complex or as simple as suits your purposes. Students really enjoy having tangible evidence of their own growth. Results of posttesting after students have been exposed to activities in creative behavior show, more often than not, dramatic increases. It's a good, positive stroke. Even if you choose only one test item and score for fluency alone, what pretesting and posttesting demonstrate to the student is worth the effort.

GROWTH CHART

Similar to the Observations of Creative Behavior Chart based on Ainsworth-Land's model that was suggested in an earlier chapter mainly for teacher use, a Growth Chart can be kept by each student. When an individual project has been completed, for example, a student can analyze the various stages of development he or she experienced throughout the process.

Growth Chart	
Formative The kinds of things I did or thought that were on the formative level.	1. 2. 3. 4. 5.
Normative The kinds of things I did or thought that were on the normative level.	1. 2. 3. 4. 5.
Integrative The kinds of things I did or thought that were on the integrative level.	1. 2. 3. 4. 5.
Transformational The kinds of things I did or thought that were on the transformational level.	1. 2. 3. 4. 5.

Another item that might be included on the Growth Chart, if appropriate, is a question in regard to making the transition from one level of development to the next. For instance, "What clues were there for you to realize that you were moving from one level to the next?" And to reinforce the part that is sometimes necessary and perfectly legitimate to go back to a previous level, "If you had to move back to a previous level, what clues let you know it was necessary?" Questions of this nature can also serve as subject matter content in the teacher's individual conference with a student.

Group work can be charted in the same way. In fact, a group's analysis of its own work can be a very valuable learning experience. For one thing, students learn a great deal from one another, as we all know. The group process helps the individual student with his or her own work. Secondly, a group of students who learn how to analyze their progress forward and occasional steps backward gain understanding of group process, more patience with one another and themselves, and a sense for the ways in which individuals contribute to group efforts.

CRITERIA SELECTION

Criteria selection for judging end products is another important phase of learning as part of evaluation in creative processes. Students sharing in the selection of criteria by which particular projects are to be evaluated expand their capacity to be selective. Criteria for group projects are determined by the group and then presented to the teacher for discussion and/or negotiation. The negotiation process helps students become keenly aware of such things as weighting certain criteria and overall fairness in judging. It is a good idea at any time to have students brainstorm possible criteria to help broaden their horizons in ways of making final judgments as fair as possible. In group work it may be determined that in addition to evaluating the success of a final product, the performance throughout the project of both the group as a whole and each individual student ought to be evaluated. In that case, sets of criteria are necessary.

For major individual projects, students can brainstorm possible criteria and then present their selections for discussion with the teacher on why and how they arrived at final selections. Students eventually become quite adept in how to measure the degree of success they have achieved in attempts to carry out their own objectives. The negotiation process with the teacher really forces students to think through their choices for criteria. Criteria should include effort as well as the quality of the end product.

CLASS ASSIGNMENTS
CARRIED OUT INDIVIDUALLY

The whole class, along with the teacher, can develop the criteria for such assignments as fun-with-a-purpose projects. Students are amazingly good at selecting suitable criteria that will cover a very broad range of interpretations of a common assignment. Typical criteria they select are

1. Uniqueness of idea
2. Thought required
3. Cleverness in use of materials
4. Time expended

FINAL RATINGS

Once the criteria and their weights have been determined, final ratings of projects can be effected through use of matrices, rating scales, or other means that seem appropriate. Another way to apply judgments based on selected criteria is by using continua. Each criterion is placed on a continuum of, say, one to nine and might look like this:
Circle the number that best represents your judgment.

	Very Poor							Excellent	
Uniqueness of idea:	1	2	3	4	5	6	7	8	9

Group work can be rated by individual members separately, with averages figured later, or the group can do the ratings collectively using a method of consensus or some other means to demonstrate group judgment.

On both group and individual work, the students, having gone through processes of criteria selection and ratings, have arrived at rather accurate assessments of their own efforts. The teacher can naturally intervene at any time if "funny business" is suspected, but students tend to take these evaluation procedures quite seriously. Students are generally pleased to be able to participate in evaluation activities and want to give a respectable performance.

INTERIM AND FINAL ASSESSMENTS

Interim and final assessments of skill development are yet another means of measuring student growth. An example of how this might be done is given using the knowledge of the elements of a problem-solving process. The example provided would be administered after the entire process has been taught and practiced. Students are asked to apply the total problem-solving process to the following situation:

> *Scott has moved to Bay City during the summer prior to his last year in junior high school. His father's job was changed, and the family had to move. His new junior high school is at least three times as big as the school he formerly attended. One of the things Scott had enjoyed most about his old school was that in both the seventh and the eighth grades he had been the class representative to the Student Council. He wants to go into politics when he grows up. He's afraid he won't be able to get involved with the Student Council in his new school because he doesn't know anybody yet. And if he isn't able to do something with the Council in the junior high, he knows he won't have any chance at all in the senior high school, since students from four different junior highs go to that school after ninth grade. School will be opening in four weeks. He saw in the school newspaper his new guidance counselor gave him when he registered that two alternate positions for Student Council representatives would be open to ninth-graders. The election is to be held at the end of September. He drools at the possibility of getting one of those positions. But how can it be done? He is new in town, doesn't know even the kids on his own block. How can he become known well enough for the kids to vote for him or, for that matter, even to get nominated?*

Now that you have read Scott's dilemma, apply the problem-solving process a step at a time as follows:

1. Define the major problem.
2. List subproblems.
3. List facts available.
4. List factual questions it would be helpful to have the answers to.

5. List possible sources for finding answers to the questions you've written.

6. Prepare a problem statement on the situation for brainstorming.

7. Brainstorm the problem for tentative solutions.

8. Develop criteria for judging the solutions.

9. Evaluate the solutions.

10. Write down what turned out to be your best solution.

11. Write a paragraph on how your solution should be implemented.

Any one of the eleven phases of the above process can be measured separately at different times, or the whole process can be presented at the same time. The teacher can go over the students' work, or students can meet in small groups to discuss and compare their individual work.

What has been emphasized throughout this discussion is the students' participation in measuring their own growth and development. Letting the students in on such things sharpens their overall ability, makes them feel important, and increases their taking responsibility for their own growth. I remember, as a college student in psychology class, wondering about myself in relation to the theories we were exposed to in the myriad of case studies we read. It seemed that everything we studied was outside the self. How I would have enjoyed learning about myself, my growth and development.

twelve

Incorporating Creative Processes into Existing Curricula

This chapter is for you to write. You know your students and you know your subject matter and now you know about creative thinking. It would be erroneous and self-defeating for me at this point to tell you precisely what to do in your classroom to evoke creative behavior. I will, however, provide some starting points and then offer some challenges.

Following are some suggested creative activities applied to specific subject matter areas:

Art
1. Have a friend draw three sample scribbles on a paper. Make a drawing out of them.
2. Sculpt something using pebbles, leaves, paste, and a paper bag.

3. Draw a picture in which you see different things by looking at it from different angles.

Health
1. Think of ways for young children to enjoy brushing their teeth.
2. Apply the problem-solving process to an antipollution campaign.
3. Write an "Easy Exercises for Lazy People" pamphlet.

Home Arts
1. Design a new kind of container or tool for your hobby.
2 Invent a meal-in-one recipe.
3. Invent a game the whole family can play.

Language Arts
1. Close your eyes and choose three words from your spelling list. Write a poem connecting the words in new ways.
2. Plan a soap opera or a mystery series by using the Morphological Approach to Story Plotting.
3. Read a story halfway through. Act out three different ways it might end.

Math
1. Think of some new ways to measure air, water, time, land, or height.
2. Devise a visual or audial way to teach a preschooler base 10.
3. Conceive of a mathematical formula based on weighted criteria for equalizing use of recess equipment, art supplies, or shared classroom duties.

Music
1. Have a friend strike three notes within an octave on a piano. Write a melody around them.
2. Invent and teach a new rhythm to the class.
3. Write some singing telegrams and deliver them to your friends or family.

Physical Education
1. Create a warm-up exercise for jogging.

2. Invent a new dance step.

3. Devise and weight criteria for arranging sports teams.

Science

1. Apply the problem-solving process to an environmental concern.

2. Use the forced-relationship technique to create new sources of energy or make new combinations of existing sources.

3. Brainstorm ways in which endangered species might be saved.

Social Studies

1. Think of new symbols that might be useful on a map.

2. Work out some solution to school problems such as lunch lines, lockers, or scheduling of the gym.

3. Brainstorm ways people of different cultures might learn to understand one another better. You might start with an attribute listing of each culture you are considering.

The foregoing suggestions might be out of context for the established curriculum in your school. Using them as possible leads, the following strategies may be of help in devising your own creative behavior activities based on the curriculum you use.

1. Add at least one objective in creative behavior to each set of objectives with which you work.

2. For each unit you teach, write three possible creative-type questions and/or creative activities that might be included.

3. Make adaptation within a unit plan to include both divergent- and convergent-thinking abilities.

4. Discuss barriers to creative expression in connection with story characters or real people in history.

5. Use the attribute-listing technique with a planned unit to see which elements of the unit best lend themselves to creative thinking.

6. Brainstorm ways in which other teachers, administrators, and parents might become supportive of incorporating creative processes into the curriculum.

7. Use a matrix as a starting point to look at all subject areas in relation to ideational techniques to spark curricular ideas.

Subject Areas	Techniques	Brainstorming	Forced Relationship	Associations	Attribute Listing
Art					
Health					
Home Arts					
Language Arts					
Math					
Music					
Physical Education					
Science					
Social Studies					

8. Use another matrix to look at ways in which problem-solving abilities might be developed through all subject areas. Then expand each relationship into a creative-type question, that is, "In what ways might I help develop students' sensitivity through art?"

Subject Areas	Problem-Solving Abilities	Developing Sensitivity	Problem Definition/ Goal Setting	Preparation	Ideation	Criteria Selection	Evaluation	Implementation
Art								
Health								
Home Arts								
Language Arts								
Math								
Music								
Physical Education								
Science								
Social Studies								

9. For units you teach that call for individual and/or group projects, consider using a creative problem-solving approach.

10. Add items to your grading system that reward creative ability such as fluency, flexibility, orginality, and elaboration.

11. Help students to measure their own growth through using the stages of development in Transformational Theory: formative, normative, integrative, transformational.

12. Have students discuss the impact of negative or positive attitudes on achievement.

What has been suggested here is the tip of the iceberg. Your own ingenuity will take over and you will enjoy some of your most rewarding teaching experiences. The foregoing ideas are intended to prod, to get you to take the first step. Go on, take it.

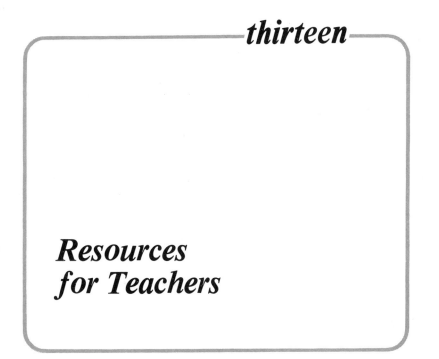

thirteen

Resources
for Teachers

This chapter is designed for those of you who would seek more information regarding creative behavior, both for your own growth and for the growth of students. The literature of creativity is extensive. The sources that appear here have been selected to supplement this book and to provide direction for the reader toward deeper investigation into the topics covered.

PERSPECTIVES IN CREATIVE BEHAVIOR

BARRON, FRANK. *Creative Person and Creative Process.* New York: Holt, Rinehart & Winston, 1969.

BARRON, FRANK. *Creativity and Personal Freedom*. London: D. Van Nostrand Company, 1968.

GHISELIN, BREWSTER. *The Creative Process*. New York: Mentor Books, 1955.

GUILFORD, J. P. *Personality*. New York: McGraw-Hill Book Company, 1959.

GUILFORD, J. P. *Way Beyond the I.Q.* Buffalo, N.Y.: Creative Education Foundation; and Great Neck, N.Y.: Creative Synergetic Associates, 1977.

JONES, P. *Creative Learning in Perspective*. London: University of London Press, 1972.

KAGAN, JEROME, ed. *Creativity and Learning*. Boston: Beacon Press, 1967.

KOESTLER, ARTHUR. *The Act of Creation*. London: Hutchinson, 1964.

LAND, GEORGE T. L. *Grow or Die: The Unifying Principle of Transformation*. New York: Dell Publishing Co., Inc., 1974.

LYTTON, HUGH. *Creativity and Education*. London: Routledge & Kegan Paul, 1971.

MACKINNON, DONALD W. *In Search of Human Effectiveness: Identifying and Developing Creativity*. Buffalo, N.Y.: Creative Education Foundation; and Great Neck, N.Y.: Creative Synergetic Associates, 1978.

MACKINNON, DONALD W. "What Makes a Person Creative?" *Saturday Review,* February 10, 1962.

MARKSBERRY, MARY LEE. *Foundations of Creativity*. New York: Harper & Row, Publishers, Inc., 1963.

PARNES, SIDNEY, and BIONDI, ANGELO. "Creative Behavior: A Delicate Balance," *Journal of Creative Behavior* 2, no. 2.

RUGG, HAROLD. *Imaginaiton*. New York: Harper & Row, Publishers, Inc., 1963.

SARTRE, JEAN-PAUL. *The Psychology of Imagination.* New York: Washington Square Press, 1966.

SHOUKSMITH, G. *Intelligence, Creativity and Cognitive Style.* London: B. T. Batsford, Ltd., 1970.

TAYLOR, I. A., and GETZELS, J. W., eds. *Perspectives in Creativity.* Chicago: Aldine Publishing Co., 1975.

TORRANCE, E. PAUL. *Education and the Creative Potential.* Minneapolis: University of Minnesota Press, 1963.

WALLACH, M. "Creativity." In Paul Mussen, ed., *Carmichael's Manual of Child Psychology.* New York: John Wiley & Sons, Inc., 1970.

EXPERIENCING
CREATIVE BEHAVIOR

ADAMS, JAMES L. *Conceptual Blockbusting: A Guide to Better Ideas.* San Francisco: W. H. Freeman & Company Publishers, 1974.

ANDREWS, MICHAEL F. *Creativity and Psychological Health.* Syracuse, N.Y.: Syracuse University Press, 1961.

CARKHUFF, R. *The Art of Problem-Solving.* Amherst, Mass.: Human Resource Development, 1973.

CRAWFORD, R. P. *Techniques of Creative Thinking.* New York: Hawthorn Books, Inc., 1954.

DAVIS, GARY. *Psychology of Problem-Solving.* New York: Basic Books, Inc., 1973.

DE BONO, EDWARD. *Lateral Thinking.* New York: Harper & Row, Publishers, Inc., 1970.

GORDON, WILLIAM J. J. *The Metaphysical Way of Learning.* Cambridge, Mass.: Synectics Education Systems, 1973.

GORDON, WILLIAM J. J. *Synergetics.* New York: Collier, 1961.

GOWAN, JOHN C. "Some New Thoughts on the Development of Creativity," *Journal of Creative Behavior* 2, no. 2.

HOLLAWAY, OTTO. *Problem-Solving: Toward a More Humanizing Curriculum.* Philadelphia: Franklin Publishing Company, 1975.

JANIS, I., and MANN, L. *Decision Making: A Psychological Analysis of Conflict, Choice, and Commitment.* New York: The Free Press, 1977.

OSBORN, ALEX F. *Applied Imagination.* 3d ed. New York: Charles Scribner's Sons, 1963.

PARNES, SIDNEY J. *Aha! Insights into Creative Behavior.* Buffalo, N.Y.: D.O.K. Publishers, 1975.

PARNES, SIDNEY J. *Creative Behavior Guidebook.* New York: Charles Scribner's Sons, 1967.

PRINCE, GEORGE. *The Practice of Creativity.* New York: Harper & Row, Publishers, Inc., 1970.

TORRANCE, E. PAUL. *The Search for Satori and Creativity.* Buffalo, N.Y.: Creative Education Foundation; and Great Neck, N.Y.: Creative Synergetic Associates, 1979.

TEACHING TO EVOKE
CREATIVE BEHAVIOR

BRAGA, JOSEPH and LAURIE. *Children and Adults: Activities for Growing Together.* Englewood Cliffs, N.J.: Prentice-Hall Publishing Co. Inc., 1976.

BRUNER, J. S. "The Conditions of Creativity." In H. E. Gruber, and others, *Contemporary Approaches to Creative Thinking.* New York: Atherton Press, 1963.

BUSWELL, G. T., and KERSH, B. Y. *Patterns of Thinking in Solving Problems.* Berkeley, Calif.: University of California Press, 1956.

DAVIS, GARY R., and DiPEGO, GERALD. *Imagination Express: Saturday Subway Ride.* Buffalo, N.Y.: D.O.K. Publishers, 1974.

DELLAS, MARIE, and GAIER, EUGENE. "Identification of Creativity: the Individual," *Psychological Bulletin* 73, no. 1 (1970).

EBERLE, ROBERT F. *Scamper: Games for Imagination Development.* Buffalo, N.Y.: D.O.K. Publishers, 1971.

GAGNE, R. M. *The Conditions of Learning.* New York: Holt, Rinehart & Winston, 1970.

GETZELS, J. W., and JACKSON, P. W., *Creativity and Intelligence: Explorations with Gifted Students.* New York: John Wiley & Sons, Inc., 1962.

GOLDMAN, R. J. "The Minnesota Tests of Creative Thinking," *Educational Research* 7, no. 1 (1964).

GOWAN, DEMOS, and TORRANCE E. PAUL, eds. *Creativity: Its Educational Implications.* New York: John Wiley & Sons, Inc., 1967.

HALL, W. B. "A Technique for Assessing Aesthetic Predispositions: Mosaic Construction Test." *Journal of Creative Behavior,* 6, no. 4, 1972.

HENDRICKS, GAY. *The Family Centering Book: Awareness Activities the Whole Family Can Do Together.* Englewood Cliffs, N.J.: Prentice-Hall Publishing Co., Inc., 1979.

HUDGINS, BRYCE B. *Problem-Solving in the Classroom.* New York: Macmillan, Inc., 1966.

KHATENA, J. "Facilitating the Creative Functions of the Gifted," *The Gifted Child Quarterly* 21, no. 2.

MEARNS, HUGHES. *Creative Power: The Education of Youth in the Creative Arts.* New York: Dover Publications, Inc., 1958.

MEDNICK, S. A. "The Remote Associates Test," *Journal of Creative Behavior* 2, no. 3 (1968).

MENLOVE, COLEEN K. *Ready, Set, Go!* Englewood Cliffs, N.J.: Prentice-Hall Publishing Co., Inc., 1978

PIAGET, J. *Play, Dreams and Imitation in Childhood.* New York: W. W. Norton & Co., Inc., 1962.

PURKEY, W. *Self-Concept and School Achievement.* Englewood Cliffs, N.J.: Prentice-Hall Publishing Co., Inc., 1970.

RICE, MARY FORMAN, and CHARLES H. FLATTER. *Help Me Learn: A Handbook for Teaching Children from Birth to Third Grade.* Englewood Cliffs, N.J.: Prentice-Hall Publishing Co., Inc., 1979.

TORRANCE, E. PAUL. "Non-test Ways of Identifying the Creatively Gifted," *Gifted Child Quarterly* 6, no. 3 (1962).

TORRANCE, E. PAUL. *Rewarding Creative Behavior.* Englewood Cliffs, N.J.: Prentice-Hall Publishing Co., Inc., 1965.

WERTHEIMER, M. *Productive Thinking.* New York: Harper, 1945.

WILLIAMS, FRANK E. *Classroom Ideas for Encouraging Thinking and Feeling.* Buffalo, N.Y.: D.O.K. Publishers, 1970.

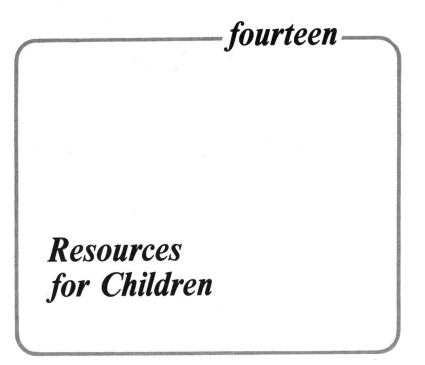

fourteen

Resources
for Children

CREATIVE THINKING SKILLS

A-Way with Problems. La Habra, Ca.: Foxtail Press, 1978.

BURNS, MARILYN. *The Book of Think.* Mountain View, Ca.: Creative Publications, 1980.

CHRISTIE, C. W. and MARAVIGLIA, F. L. *Creative Problem-Solving Thinkbook.* Buffalo, N.Y.: DOK Publishers, Inc., 1974.

DAVIS, GARY. *Imagination Express.* Buffalo, N.Y.: DOK Publishers, Inc., 1972.

Detecting and Deducing. La Habra, Ca.: Foxtail Press, 1978.

EBERLE, B. and STANISH, BOB. *CPS for Kids.* Buffalo, N.Y.: DOK Publishers, Inc., 1980.

EBERLE, BOB. *Scamper.* Buffalo, N.Y.: DOK Publishers, Inc., 1971.

Elaborative Thinking. Woburn, Ma.: Curriculum Associates, 1976.

KING, JOYCE and KATZMAN, CAROL. *Imagine That!* Pacific Palisades, Ca.: Goodyear Publishing Co., Inc., 1976.

MOHAN, MADAN and RISKO, VICTORIA. *Why Knots!* Buffalo, N.Y.: DOK Publishers, Inc., 1979.

RAUDSEPP, EUGENE. *Creative Growth Games.* New York: Jove Publications, Inc., 1977.

SANGER, SISTER GREGORY. *Ladybug Helps Teach the Five Senses.* Buffalo, N.Y.: DOK Publishers, Inc., 1971.

SEUSS, DR. *Oh! The Thinks You Can Think!* Westminster, Md.: Random House, Inc., 1975.

Synectics Inc. *Making It Strange: A New Design for Creative Thinking and Writing, Books 1, 2, 3, 4.* Scranton, Pa.: Harper and Row Publishers, Inc., 1968.

THINK-INS. Monterey Park, Ca.: Creative Teaching Press, Inc., 1974.

Thinklab. Chicago, Il.: Science Research Associates, Inc., 1977.

WOLF, JANET and OWETT, B. *Let's Imagine Thinking Up Things.* New York: E.P. Dutton and Co., Inc., 1961.

WOODS, MARGARET S. *Wonderwork: Creative Experiences for the Young Child.* Buffalo, N.Y.: DOK Publishers, Inc., 1970.

PERCEPTIONS AND PERSPECTIVES

COHEN, DANIEL. *The World's Most Famous Ghosts.* New York: Pocket Books, 1979.

DE MILLE, RICHARD. *Put Your Mother on the Ceiling.* New York: Penguin Books, 1976.

GILMAN, RITA G. and SELIGSON, MARCIA. *UFO Encounters.* Englewood Cliffs, N.J.: Scholastic Book Services, 1978.

KOHL, JUDITH and KOHL, HERBERT. *The View from the Oak: The Private Worlds of Other Creatures.* New York: Charles Scribner's Sons, 1978.

MITSUMASA, ANNO. *Topsy-Turvies: Pictures to Stretch the Imagination.* Rutland, Vt.: Weatherhill, 1970.

MOHAN, MADAN and RISKO, VICTORIA. *Perception Stimulators.* Buffalo, N.Y.: DOK Publishers, Inc., 1979.

SEYMOUR, DALE and SEYMOUR, MARGO. *Perceptual Puzzle Blocks.* Mountain Valley, Ca.: Creative Publications, 1980.

STEVENS, PETER S. *Patterns in Nature.* Mountain View, Ca.: Creative Publications, 1978.

WENTZELL, MELINDA and HOLLAND, D. K. *Optricks.* San Francisco, Ca.: Troubador Press, 1973.

GAMES THAT CHALLENGE

ALLEN, LAYMAN E. *Equations: The Game of Creative Mathematics.* Ann Arbor, Mi.: Wff 'N Proof Games, 1978.

_____ *Wff 'N Proof: The Game of Modern Logic.* Ann Arbor, Mi.: Wff 'N Proof Games, 1976.

_____, GOODMAN, FREDERICK L., HUMPHREY, DORIS and ROSS, JOAN. *On-Words: The Game of Word Structures.* Ann Arbor, Mi.: Wff 'N Proof Games, 1979.

————, KUGEL, PETER and OWENS, MARTIN. *On-Sets: The Game of Set Theory*. Ann Arbor, Mi.: Wff 'N Proof Games, 1979.

————, ROSS, JOAN and KUGEL, PETER. *Queries and Theories: The Game of Science and Language*. Ann Arbor, Mi.: Wff 'N Proof Games, 1977.

American Dream. Springfield, Ma.: Milton Bradley Company, 1980.

Bandits of Natchez Trace Puzzle. Savannah, Tn.: Parris Manufacturing Company, 1980.

Boggle. Beverly, Ma.: Parker Brothers, 1976.

Brain Baffler. Hawthorne, Ca.: Mattel Electronics, 1980.

Can't Stop. Beverly, Ma.: Parker Brothers, 1980.

Catch a Thief. San Francisco, Ca.: Knots, Inc., 1980.

Click and Clasp: Construction Toys. Stamford, Ct.: Click, Ltd., 1980.

Computer Gin. Hawthorne, Ca.: Mattel Electronics, 1980.

Connect Four. Springfield, Ma.: Milton Bradley Company, 1975.

Decipher. New York: Pressman Toy Corp., 1978.

Dragon Chinese Checkers. Springfield, Ma.: Milton Bradley Company, 1980.

Ergo. New York: Invicta Plastics (U.S.A.), Ltd., 1978.

Flash Gordon Space Game. Hawthorne, Ca.: Mattel Electronics, 1980.

Foreign Exchange. Baltimore, Md.: The Avalon Hill Game Company, 1977.

GREEN, LORNE and ALLEN, ROBERT. *The Propaganda Game*. Ann Arbor, Mi.: Wff 'N Proof Games, 1979.

Hangman. Springfield, Ma.: Milton Bradley Company, 1974.

Hexed. Hagerstown, Md.: Gabriel CBS Toys, Division of CBS, Inc., 1978.

Hi-Q. Hagerstown, Md.: Gabriel CBS Toys, Division of CBS, Inc., 1978.

The Hobbit Game. Springfield, Ma.: Milton Bradley Company, 1978.

I Took a Lickin' from a Chicken. New York: L.J.N. Toys, 1980.

Kismet. Minneapolis, Mn.: Lakeside Games, 1978.

Lord of the Rings, The. Springfield, Ma.: Milton Bradley Company, 1978.

Master Mind. New York: Invicta Plastics (U.S.A.), Ltd., 1976.

Matrix. San Francisco, Ca.: Knots, Inc., 1980.

Mental Blok Puzzle. Savannah, Tn.: Parris Manufacturing Company, 1979.

Pythagoras. Hagerstown, Md.: Gabriel CBS Toys, Division of CBS, Inc., 1978.

Restack 'em Puzzle. Savannah, Tn.: Parris Manufacturing Company, 1979.

Reverse 'em Puzzle. Savannah, Tn.: Parris Manufacturing Company, 1980.

Spill and Spell. Beverly, Ma.: Parker Brothers, 1971.

Spirograph. Cincinnati, Oh.: Kenner Products, 1971.

Stay Alive. Springfield, Ma.: Milton Bradley Company, 1978.

Stratego. Springfield, Ma.: Milton Bradley Company, 1969.

Super Simon. Springfield, Ma.: Milton Bradley Company, 1979.

Superperfection. Minneapolis, Mn.: Lakeside Games, 1976.

Tick Tack Math. Campbell, Ca.: Rules of the Road, 1977.

TRIAD: The Strategic Game of Pharoahs and Kings. Chattanooga, Tn.: T & M Enterprises, Inc., 1979.

Uno. Joliet, Il.: International Games, 1979.

Yahtzee. Springfield, Ma.: Milton Bradley Company, 1972.

PUZZLES AND RIDDLES

BARRY, SHEILA A. *A Super-Colossal Book of Puzzles, Tricks, and Games.* New York: Sterling Publishing Co., Inc., 1978.

Brain Scratchers. Phoenix, Az.: Resources for the Gifted, 1979.

BROOKE, MAXEY. *Coin Games and Puzzles.* Mountain View, Ca.: Creative Publications, 1980.

HULL, JOHN. *Puzzlers.* San Francisco, Ca.: Troubador Press, 1974.

LOW, JOSEPH. *A Mad Wet Hen and Other Riddles.* West Caldwell, N.J.: Greenwillow Books, William Morrow & Co., Inc., 1977.

MIKLOWITZ, GLORIA D. and DESBERG, PETER. *Ghastly Ghostly Riddles.* Englewood Cliffs, N.J.: Scholastic Book Services, 1978.

Mind Benders. Troy, Mi.: Midwest Publications Co., Inc., 1979.

SCHWARTZ, ALVIN. *A Twister of Twists, A Tangler of Tongues.* New York: Bantam Books, Inc., 1976.

SCHWARTZ, ALVIN. *Tomfoolery: Trickery and Foolery with Words.* New York: Bantam Books, Inc., 1977.

SUMMERS, GEORGE J. *Mind Teasers: Logic Puzzles and Games of Deduction.* New York: Sterling Publishing Co., Inc., 1977.

Survival Skills. Phoenix, Az.: Resources for the Gifted, 1979.

THALER, MIKE. *Never Tickle a Turtle: Cartoons, Riddles and Funny Stories.* New York: Franklin Watts, Inc., 1977.

TIGO Games. Spartanburg, S.C.: Ward and Sons. 1979.

TIGO Puzzles. Spartanburg, S.C.: Ward and Sons, 1979.

DO IT YOURSELF

ABISCH, ROZ. *The Make-It, Play-It Game Book.* New York: Walker and Company, 1974.

ARNESON, DON. *Doing Something Nice* and *Other Short Plays for Kids.* Burnsville, Mn.: Bookmaker Publishing, 1979.

BALZER, JOHN A. *Fabulous Freaky Fun Fill-Ins for Fridays.* Buffalo, N.Y.: DOK Publishers, Inc., 1979.

BENTLEY, W. A. and HUMPHREYS, W. J. *Snow Crystals.* Mountain View, Ca.: Creative Publications, 1976.

BRANDENBERG, FRANTZ. *What Can You Make of It?* West Caldwell, N.J.: Greenwillow Books, William Morrow & Co., Inc., 1977.

CARAWAY, CAREN. *The Beginner's Guide to Quilting.* New York: David McKay Company, Inc., 1980.

Cartloads of Creative Story Starters. Clinton, Oh.: Carson Dellosa, Inc., 1976.

CHEATHAM, VAL R. *Cartooning for Kids Who Draw and Kids Who Don't Draw.* Buffalo, N.Y.: DOK Publishers, Inc., 1979.

CIVARDI, ANNE, ed. *The Know How Book of Action Games: Lots of Simple Games to Make and Play.* New York: Sterling Publishing Company, Inc., 1976.

COLE, W. and COLMORE, JULIA, ed. *The Poetry-Drawing Book.* New York: Simon and Schuster, Inc., 1960.

Compoz-a Puzzle. Sea Cliff, N.Y., Composition Press, Inc., 1979.

CORWIN, JUDITH HOFFMAN. *Creative Collage.* New York: David McKay Co., Inc., 1980.

COSNER, SHARON. *Masks Around the World and How to Make Them.* New York: David McKay Co., Inc., 1979.

CROSBY, NINA E. and MARTEN, ELIZABETH H. *Don't Teach! Let Me Learn!* Buffalo, N.Y.: DOK Publishers, Inc., 1979.

Crystal Honeycomb Cut-Out Kit. Middletown, Oh.: The Crystal Tissue Company, 1976.

CUMMINGS, RICHARD. *Be Your Own Detective: How to Conduct Investigations and Make Basic Equipment.* New York: David McKay Co., Inc., 1980.

_____. *Fun with Monsters: Create Your Own Masks, Make-Up, and Props.* New York: David McKay Co., Inc., 1979.

_____. *Make Your Own Alternative Energy.* New York: David McKay Co., Inc., 1979.

Decide and Design. Phoenix, Az.: Resources for the Gifted, 1979.

DEREGNIERS, BEATRICE S. *What Can You Do With A Shoe?* Harper and Row Publishers, Inc., 1978.

EAGLE, ARNOLD. *Beginner's Guide to Super 8 Film Making.* New York: David McKay Co., Inc., 1980.

ELLEFSON, LINDA. *Say It with Movement.* Buffalo, N.Y.: DOK Publishers, Inc., 1973.

GRAHAM, ADA. *Foxtails, Ferns, and Fish Scales: A Handbook of Art and Nature Projects.* New York: Four Winds Press, 1977.

HAAS, CAROLYN. *The Big Book of Recipes for Fun.* Northfield, Il.: CBH Publishing, Inc., 1980.

Kelly's String and Wire Art Kits. Cincinnati, Oh.: Kelly's String Art, 1978.

KRAUSS, RUTH. *Little King, Little Queen, Little Monster, and Other Stories You Can Make Up Yourself.* Englewood Cliffs, N.J.: Scholastic Book Services, 1969.

LIDSTONE, JOHN and MCINTOSH, DON. *Children as Film Makers.* New York: Van Nostrand Reinhold Company, 1979.

LITTLE, LESSIE JONES and GREENFIELD, ELOISE. *I Can Do It By Myself. New York: Thomas Y. Crowell Company, 1978.*

LOPSHIRE, ROBERT. *How to Make Snop Snappers and Other Fine Things.* West Caldwell, N.J.: Greenwillow Books, William Morrow & Co., Inc., 1976.

MCCASLIN, NELLIE. *Shows on a Shoestring: An Easy Guide to Amateur Productions.* New York: David McKay Co., Inc., 1979.

MCGRATH, RUTH EHRIG and GRAHAM, BETH G. *Tools, Wood and Glue: An Invitation to Grow.* Buffalo, N.Y.: DOK Publishers, Inc., 1977.

Makit Kits Series. Dallas, Tx.: Makit Products, Inc., 1977.

PARISH, PEGGY. *Sheet Magic: Games, Toys, and Gifts from Old Sheets.* Riverside, N.J.: Macmillan Publishing Co., Inc., 1971.

Placemats: Personalized. Westfield, N.J.: Matmaker Company, 1980.

Pumpkins, Pinwheels, and Peppermint Packages (Student Edition). Nashville, Tn.: Incentive Publications, Inc., 1977.

SEIDELMAN, JAMES E. *Creating with Paint.* New York: Macmillan Publishing Co., Inc., 1967.

SEVERN, BILL. *Bill Severn's Big Book of Magic.* New York: David McKay Co., Inc., 1980.

_____. *Bill Severn's Guide to Magic as a Hobby.* New York: David McKay Co., Inc., 1979.

_____. *50 Ways to Have Fun with Old Newspapers.* New York: David McKay Co., Inc., 1980.

_____. *Magic in Your Pockets.* New York: David McKay Co., Inc., 1974.

SMITH, ROBERT T. *Make a Wish Come True.* Mankato, Mn.: Creative Education, Inc., 1973.

Story Starters. Monterey Park, Ca.: Creative Teaching Press, Inc., 1974.

THORNTON, ALBERTA G. "You Can Write Haiku." Chicago, Il.: *Highlights: The Monthly Book for Children,* May 1965, pp. 36-37.

TODD, LEONARD. *Trash Can Toys and Games.* New York: Penguin Books, Inc., 1976.

WEBSTER, JAMES. *Toys and Games to Make.* Bedford Hills, N.Y.: Merry Thoughts, 1969.

ZECHLIN, KATHARINA. *Games You Can Build Yourself.* New York: Sterling Publishing Co., Inc., 1975.

ZULIANA, VILMA. *I Believe in Make-Believe.* Chicago, Il.: Follett Corporation, 1977.

FICTION: FANTASY, IMAGINATION, PROBLEM-SOLVING, AND SENSITIVITY

ALLARD, HARRY. *Miss Nelson Is Missing.* Englewood Cliffs, N.J.: Scholastic Book Services, 1978.

ANNO, MISUMASA. *Anno's Journey.* Cleveland, Oh.: William Collins, + World Publishing Co., Inc., 1978.

ARTHUR, ROBERT. *Alfred Hitchcock and the Three Investigators in the Mystery of the Talking Skull.* Westminster, Md.: Random House, Inc., 1978.

ATWATER, RICHARD and ATWATER, FLORENCE. *Mr. Popper's Penguins.* New York: Dell Publishing Co., Inc., 1978.

BACH, ALICE. *Mollie Make-Believe.* Scranton, Pa.: Harper and Row Publishers, Inc., 1974.

BARRETT, JUDY. *Cloudy with a Chance of Meatballs.* Paterson, N.J.: Atheneum Publishers, 1978.

BISHOP, CLAIRE HUCHET. *Twenty and Ten.* New York: Puffin Books, 1978.

BOND, MICHAEL and BRADLEY, ALFRED. *Paddington on Stage.* New York: Dell Publishing Co., Inc., 1978.

BRADLEY, MICHAEL. *The Shaping Room.* New York: Dodd, Mead & Company, 1978.

BRAM, ELIZABETH. *One Day I Closed My Eyes and the World Disappeared.* New York: The Dial Press, 1978.

BURNINGHAM, JOHN. *Come Away from the Water, Shirley.* New York: Thomas Y. Crowell Company, 1978.

BURTON, VIRGINIA LEE. *The Little House.* Boston, Ma.: Houghton Mifflin Company, 1978.

BUTTERWORTH, OLIVER. *The Enormous Egg.* New York: Dell Publishing Co., Inc., 1978.

CHAPMAN, CAROL. *Barney Bipple's Magic Dandelion.* New York: E.P. Dutton and Co., Inc.,

COLBY, CURTIS. *Bill's Great Idea.* St. Paul, Mn.: EMC Corporation, 1973.

CONE, MOLLY. *Call Me Moose.* Boston, Ma.: Houghton Mifflin Company, 1978.

CURRY, JANE. *Daybreakers.* New York: Harcourt Brace Jovanovich, Inc., 1970.

DAYRELL, ELPHINSTONE. *Why the Sun and the Moon Live in the Sky.* Boston, Ma.: Houghton Mifflin Company, 1976.

DIVEN, ANNE. *The Scribner Anthology for Young People.* New York: Charles Scribner's Sons, 1977.

ERICKSON, RUSSELL E. *Warton and Morton.* West Caldwell, N.J.: William Morrow and Co., Inc., 1977.

FIFE, DALE. *North of Danger.* Greensboro, N.C.: Unicorn Press, 1978.

FIRST, JULIA. *Move Over, Beethoven.* New York: Franklin Watts, Inc., 1978.

GACKENBACH, DICK. *Mother Rabbit's Son Tom.* New York: Harper and Row, Publishers, Inc., 1977.

GREENE, CONSTANCE C. and McCULLY, EMILY A. *Isabelle the Itch.* New York: Dell Publishing Co., Inc., 1974.

GWYNNE, FRED. *A Chocolate Moose for Dinner.* New York: Windmill Books and E.P. Dutton and Co., Inc., 1976.

HILDRICK, E. W. *The Case of the Secret Scribbler.* New York: Pocket Books, 1979.

———. *The McGurk Mystery Series.* New York: Pocket Books Education Department, 1976.

HOLL, ADELAIDE. *If We Could Make Wishes.* Champaign, Il.: Garrad Publishing Co., 1977.

JEFFERS, SUSAN. *Wild Robin.* New York: E.P. Dutton and Co., Inc., 1976.

JENSEN, VIRGINIA ALLEN. *Sara and the Door.* Reading, Ma.: Children's Book Dept., Addison-Wesley Publishing Co., Inc., 1977.

KELLER, BEVERLY. *The Beetle Bush.* New York: Dell Publishing Co., Inc., 1978.

KENNEDY, RICHARD. *Oliver Hyde's Dishcloth Concert.* Boston, Ma.: Little, Brown & Company, 1976.

KEY, ALEXANDER. *The Case of the Vanishing Boy.* New York: Pocket Books, 1979.

KIMBALL, RICHARD L. *A Search for the Great White Also.* San Leandro, Ca.: Educational Science Consultants, 1974.

KING, CLIVE. *Stig of the Dump.* New York: Viking Press, Inc., 1978.

KRAHN, FERNANDO. *The Family Minus.* New York: Parents' Magazine Press, 1977.

KUBINYI, LASZLO. *Zeki and the Talking Cat Shukru.* New York: Simon and Schuster, Inc., 1970.

L'ENGLE, MADELEINE. *A Swiftly Tilting Planet.* New York: Farrar, Straus & Giroux, Inc., 1978.

LENSKI, LOIS. *Lois Lenski's Big Book of Mr. Small.* New York: David McKay Co., Inc., 1979.

LEROY, GENE. *Emma's Dilemma.* New York: Harper and Row, Publishers, Inc., 1977.

_____. *Hotheads.* New York: Harper and Row, Publishers, Inc., 1977.

MARSHALL, JAMES. *George and Martha Encore.* Boston, Ma.: Houghton Mifflin Company, 1977.

MARZOLLA, JEAN. *Close Your Eyes.* New York: The Dial Press, 1978.

MERRIAM, EVE. *What Can You Do with a Pocket?* Westminster, Md.: Alfred A. Knopf, Inc., 1964.

O'NEILL, MARY. *Hailstones and Halibut Bones.* New York: Doubleday & Co., Inc., 1961.

PAPE, DONNA L. *A Bone for Breakfast.* Champaign, Il.: Garrad Publishing Co., 1974.

PEET, BILL. *Wump World.* Boston, Ma.: Houghton Mifflin Company, 1970.

PENE DuBOIS, WILLIAM. *Otto and the Magic Potatoes.* New York: Viking Press, Inc., 1970.

RASKIN, ELLEN. *The Westing Game.* New York: E. P. Dutton and Co., Inc., 1978.

RAYNER, MARY. *Garth Pig and the Ice Cream Lady.* Paterson, N.J.: Atheneum Publishers, 1978.

REY, H. A. *Cecily G. and the Nine Monkeys.* Boston, Ma.: Houghton Mifflin Company, 1975.

ROBINSON, JEAN. *Secret Life of T.K. Dearing.* Somers, Ct.: Seabury Press, Inc., 1973.

ROSEN, WINIFRED. *Henrietta and the Day of the Iguana.* Englewood Cliffs, N.J.: Four Winds Press, 1978.

SAUER, JULIA LINA. *Fog Magic.* New York: Pocket Books, Inc., 1976.

SHARMAT, MARJORIE WEINMAN. *Nate the Great Goes Undercover.* New York: Dell Publishing Co., Inc., 1978.

SILVERSTEIN, SHEL. *Where the Sidewalk Ends.* New York: Harcourt Brace Jovanovich, Inc., 1974.

SOBOL, DONALD J. *Encyclopedia Brown Series.* New York: Pocket Books, 1975.

STUART, JESSE. *Come to My Tomorrowland.* Nashville, Tn.: Aurora Publications, 1971.

THAYER, JANE. *Andy and Mr. Cunningham.* Caldwell, N.J.: William Morrow & Co., Inc., 1969.

TOLAN, STEPHANIE S. *Grandpa and Me.* New York: Charles Scribner's Sons, 1978.

TRUSE, KENNETH. *Benny's Magic Baking Pan.* Champaign, Il.: Garrad Publishing Co., 1974.

UNADA, GLIEWE. *Andrew's Amazing Boxes.* East Rutherford, N.J.: G. P. Putnam's Sons, 1971.

WABER, BERNARD. *Lovable Lyle.* Boston, Ma.: Houghton Mifflin Company, 1976.

WILLIAMS, JAY. *The Reward Worth Having.* New York: Four Winds Press, 1976.

WILSON, GAHAN. *Harry, The Fat Bear Spy.* New York: Dell Publishing Co., Inc., 1978.

_____. *Harry and the Sea Serpent.* New York: Dell Publishing Co., Inc., 1978.

WINDSOR, PATRICIA. *Mad Martin.* Scranton, Pa.: Harper and Row, Publishers, Inc., 1978.

WOLITZER, HILMA. *Introducing Shirley Braverman.* New York: Dell Publishing Co., Inc., 1978.

WYLER, ROSE and AMES, GERALD. *Magic Secrets.* Scranton, Pa.: Harper and Row, Publishers, Inc., 1978.

YEP, LAURENCE. *Child of the Owl.* New York: Harper and Row, Publishers, Inc., 1977.

Bibliography

ALLEN, M.S. *Morphological Creativity.* Englewood Cliffs, N.J.: Prentice-Hall Publishing Co., 1962.

BARRON, F. *Creative Person and Creative Process.* New York: Holt, Rinehart & Winston, 1969.

BARRON, F. *Creativity and Personal Freedom.* London: D. Van Nostrand Company, 1968.

BELCHER, T., and RUBOVITZ, J. "The Measurement of Creativity: Interrelations Among Ten Different Creativity Tests." *Journal of Creative Behavior* 2, no. 3.

BIANCHI, MARTHA DICKINSON, and HAMPSON, ALFRED LEETE, eds. *Poems by Emily Dickinson.* Boston: Little, Brown & Company, 1957.

CRAWFORD, R. P. *The Techniques of Creative Thinking.* New York: Hawthorn Books, Inc., 1954.

DAVIS, GARY A. *It's Your Imagination: Theory and Training of Problem-Solving.* New York: Basic Books, 1972.

GALTON, F. *Hereditary Genius: An Inquiry into Its Laws and Consequences.* New York: Appleton, 1869.

GHISELIN, B. *The Creative Process.* New York: Mentor Books, 1955.

GUILFORD, J. P. *Way Beyond the I.Q.* Buffalo, N.Y.: Creative Education Foundation; and Great Neck, N.Y.: Creative Synergetic Associates, 1977.

LAND, G. T. L. *Grow or Die: The Unifying Principle of Transformation.* New York: Dell Publishing Co., Inc., 1973.

LEHMAN, H. C. *Age and Achievement.* Princeton, N.J.: Princeton Univ. Press, 1953.

MACKINNON, D. W. *In Search of Human Effectiveness: Identifying and Developing Creativity.* Buffalo, N.Y.: Creative Education Foundation; and Great Neck, N.Y.: Creative Synergetic Associates, 1978.

MACKINNON, D. W. "What Makes a Person Creative." *Saturday Review,* February 10, 1962.

MARKBERRY, M. L. *Foundations of Creativity.* New York: Harper & Row, Publishers, Inc., 1963.

MASLOW, A. *Motivation and Personality.* New York: Harper & Row, Publishers, Inc., 1954.

The Merriam-Webster Dictionary. New York: Pocket Books, 1979.

OSBORN, A. F. *Applied Imagination.* 3d rev. ed. New York: Charles Scribner's Sons, 1963.

PARNES, S. J. *Creative Behavior Guidebook.* New York: Charles Scribner's Sons, 1967.

PARNES, S. J., and HARDING, H. F. eds. *A Source Book for Creative Thinking*. New York: Charles Scribner's Sons, 1962.

PATRICK, C. "Whole and Part Relationship in Creative Thought," *American Journal of Psychology*. 1944, 54, 128–131.

PERLS, F. *Gestalt Therapy Verbatim*. Lafayette, Calif.: Real People Press, 1969.

ROSSMAN, J. *The Psychology of the Inventor*. Washington, D.C.: Inventors Publishing Co., 1931.

SHALLCROSS, D. J. "Creative Problem-Solving." *High School English Notes*. Boston: Ginn and Company, 1969.

SHALLCROSS, D. J. "Creative Problem-Solving at Cleveland Heights High School." *Michigan Journal of Secondary Education,* Winter 1969.

SHALLCROSS, D. J. "Creative Problem-Solving in High School." *National Education Association Journal.* (now *Today's Education*) (Washington, D.C.), March 1967.

SHALLCROSS, D. J. "Creativity: Everybody's Business." *Personnel and Guidance Journal,* May 1973.

SHALLCROSS, D. J. "Creativity Course in High School." *Education Digest,* Fall 1967.

SHALLCROSS, D. J. *Course Guide to Teaching Creative Problem-Solving*. Cleveland Heights, Ohio: Board of Education, 1966.

SHALLCROSS, D. J. "Developing Creative Potential through a Course in Creative Problem-Solving." *The Bulletin of the National Association of Secondary School Principals,* March 1971.

SHALLCROSS, D. J. "Education Is . . . " In Oswald Swallow, ed., *Management Perspectives for Economic Development and Human Welfare*. Johannesburg, South Africa: Management Research Institute, Ltd., 1979.

SHALLCROSS, D. J. "First High School Creativity Course." *Ohio Schools.* (Columbus, Ohio), November 1965.

SHALLCROSS, D. J. *Implementing Psychological Curriculum: An Investigation of the Instructional Concerns of Teachers.* Ph.D. dissertation, University of Massachusetts, 1973.

SHALLCROSS, D. J. "Solution de Problems." *Saber,* October 1967.

SHALLCROSS, D. J., and others. *Ingredients Project: A Curriculum Guide for Humanistic Education.* Turners Falls, Mass.: Montague Public Schools, May 1973.

TORRANCE, E. P. *Guiding Creative Talent.* Englewood Cliffs, N.J.: Prentice-Hall Publishing Co., Inc., 1964.

WALLAS, G. *The Art of Thought.* London: C. A. Watts, 1945.

WALLACH, M. A. and KOGAN, N. *Modes of Thinking in Young Children.* New York: Holt, 1965.

Webster's Seventh New Collegiate Dictionary. Springfield, Mass.: G. and C. Merriam Company, 1963.

WHITING, C. S. *Creative Thinking.* New York: Reinhold Publishing Corporation, 1958.

Index

167